SpringerBriefs in Finance

SpringerBriefs present concise summaries of cutting-edge research and practical applications across a wide spectrum of fields. Featuring compact volumes of 50 to 125 pages, the series covers a range of content from professional to academic. Typical topics might include: a timely report of state-of-the art analytical techniques, a bridge between new research results, as published in journal articles, and a contextual literature review, a snapshot of a hot or emerging topic, an in-depth case study or clinical example, and a presentation of core concepts that students must understand in order to make independent contributions. SpringerBriefs in Finance showcase emerging theory, empirical research, and practical application in corporate finance, banking, financial management, behavioral finance, financial markets, social and entrepreneurial finance, microfinance, and related fields, from a global author community. Briefs are characterized by fast, global electronic dissemination, standard publishing contracts, standardized manuscript preparation and formatting guidelines, and expedited production schedules.

Luca Barbaro · Daniele Previtali · Roberto Rosato

Crypto and Decentralized Finance Under Stress

A Comprehensive Risk Assessment of Vulnerabilities and Attack Techniques

Springer

Luca Barbaro
Parthenope University of Naples
Naples, Italy

Daniele Previtali
Parthenope University of Naples
Naples, Italy

Roberto Rosato
Zug, Switzerland

ISSN 2193-1720 ISSN 2193-1739 (electronic)
SpringerBriefs in Finance
ISBN 978-3-032-28424-2 ISBN 978-3-032-28425-9 (eBook)
https://doi.org/10.1007/978-3-032-28425-9

This work was partially supported by project SHIELD (CUP: B53C22003990006) within the research program PE 'Security and Rights in the CyberSpace—SERICS' (PE00000014) under the MUR National Recovery and Resilience Plan funded by the European Union—NextGenerationEU.

This Springer imprint is published by the registered company Springer Nature Switzerland AG
The registered company address is: Gewerbestrasse 11, 6330 Cham, Switzerland

Acknowledgements The authors are deeply grateful to Riccardo Caracci for his contribution to this work, particularly for conducting the data collection and part of the empirical analyses, from which this monograph has significantly benefited.

Competing Interests The authors have no competing interests to declare that are relevant to the content of this manuscript.

Introduction

Distributed Ledger Technology (DLT)[1] has increasingly been discussed as a foundational infrastructure for the digital transformation of financial services, with both potential benefits and challenges for market organization and risk management (Leo and Panetta, 2023; CPMI, 2017). In this setting, decentralized finance (DeFi) has emerged as a rapidly evolving ecosystem of crypto-asset services enabled by smart contracts[2] deployed on blockchains and protocol-based coordination. The DeFi paradigm allows for the execution of trading, lending, payments, and other financial services without the need for traditional intermediaries. It thereby replicates several core services of traditional finance (TradFi) while reconfiguring the way financial coordination, accountability, and enforcement are achieved (Aramonte et al., 2021; FSB, 2024). This new paradigm has attracted a growing community of both users and developers, and it has also generated new forms of fragility. In contrast to institution-centered finance, where governance, risk controls, and legal accountability are anchored in regulated entities, DeFi relies on protocol design choices and technical infrastructures that operationalize trust among participants. Therefore, vulnerabilities may originate from market misconduct and structural weaknesses in the underlying infrastructure, such as deficiencies in software implementation, flawed incentive mechanisms, and inter-protocol dependencies.

The rise of decentralized finance (DeFi) has coincided with pronounced volatility and recurrent boom-and-bust cycles in crypto-asset markets (Aramonte et al., 2021; IMF, 2022). Periods of rapid expansion have been followed by sharp contractions, often triggered by confidence shocks, governance failures, technical vulnerabilities, or the destabilization of key crypto-assets. These dynamics have generated

[1] Distributed ledger technologies (DLTs) refer to a class of systems that enable the recording, sharing, and updating of data across a network of distributed nodes; blockchain-based systems are a prominent subset of DLT implementations. (See CPMI/BIS, 2017, for an institutional overview of DLT in payment, clearing, and settlement).

[2] The smart contract is a self-executing program registered on the blockchain that automatically implements clauses and conditions defined in the code. Written in specific languages (such as Solidity), it operates without intermediaries, ensuring deterministic execution, transparency and immutability.

substantial gains for some participants and significant losses for others, particularly retail investors, during episodes of market stress commonly referred to as "crypto winters".[3] Beyond their distributional effects, the systemic relevance of DeFi has grown as crypto markets expanded and became increasingly interconnected with the broader financial system, both directly and indirectly.

In response, regulators and international standard-setting bodies, including IOSCO, the Financial Stability Board, and central banks, have intensified their assessment of crypto-related risks, market integrity concerns, and consumer protection challenges (FSB, 2024; Bank of England, 2022). While early regulatory responses largely reflected a wait-and-see approach, given the sector's initially limited scale, the magnitude and complexity of recent disruptions have underscored the need for more structured supervisory frameworks and policy intervention. More recent analytical work confirms a gradual shift toward a comprehensive, risk-based regulatory stance. The 2025 Joint EBA-ESMA Report highlights that, although DeFi remains a niche segment in terms of total value locked, it exhibits structural vulnerabilities that warrant supervisory attention, particularly in the areas of ICT risk, smart contract exploitation, governance attacks, and off-chain weaknesses such as private key compromise (EBA–ESMA, 2025). The same report identifies significant money-laundering and terrorist-financing risks stemming from pseudonymity, the absence of effective AML/CFT controls at protocol level, and the cross-border, permissionless architecture of decentralized exchanges. In parallel, DeFi lending and borrowing models generate financial stability concerns through collateral chains, rehypothecation, and procyclical liquidation dynamics, with the potential for cascade liquidations and liquidity spirals across interconnected protocols (EBA–ESMA, 2025). At the global level, the International Monetary Fund (IMF) and the Financial Stability Board (FSB) stress that, while crypto-asset markets remain small relative to global financial assets, their growing interlinkages with traditional finance may amplify systemic risk if left unaddressed (IMF–FSB, 2024). Particular attention is devoted to cross-border regulatory arbitrage, non-compliance, and the challenges posed by offshore activity, which undermine the effectiveness of fragmented national approaches. The IMF further emphasizes that stablecoins, often embedded in DeFi liquidity and settlement infrastructures, can create macrofinancial vulnerabilities, including run dynamics, fire-sale externalities in reserve assets, currency substitution, and volatile capital flows, especially in emerging market and developing economies (IMF, 2025). Accordingly, the regulatory trajectory is evolving from exploratory monitoring toward the construction of structured supervisory frameworks centered on financial stability, consumer protection, market integrity, operational resilience, and macrofinancial safeguards. In the European Union, MiCAR explicitly mandates an assessment of the feasibility and necessity of regulating decentralized systems and crypto lending and borrowing, while EBA and ESMA continue systematic monitoring to inform potential supervisory or legislative action (EBA–ESMA, 2025). At the international level, the IMF–FSB Roadmap promotes coordinated implementation of global standards, enhanced data collection, and cross-border cooperation

[3] https://www.bloomberg.com/features/2023-crypto-winter/.

(IMF–FSB, 2024). The emerging approach therefore reflects a transition from regulatory forbearance to a structured, multi-layered governance framework aimed at internalizing the externalities generated by DeFi within the broader financial system. Considering these developments, understanding the sources and propagation mechanisms of vulnerabilities in DeFi has become a core challenge for policymakers, market participants, and researchers.

This book adopts the perspective that many recurring weaknesses in decentralized finance are not merely incidental anomalies but are linked to deeper structural features of protocol-based financial intermediation. DeFi does not eliminate intermediation, rather, it relocates it. Functions traditionally performed by regulated institutions (e.g., screening, custody, market making, settlement finality, and dispute resolution) are partially decomposed and reassembled across smart contracts, governance systems, off-chain service providers, and boundary infrastructures (e.g., bridges, oracles, and privacy-enhancing tools). This shift reshapes in a way the meaning of trust: instead of being primarily anchored in institutions and legal enforceability, trust increasingly depends on code correctness, economic incentives, governance legitimacy, and the reliability of supporting infrastructures. This conceptual lens helps explain why certain categories of risk, particularly operational, technological, and governance-related vulnerabilities, can have outsized consequences in DeFi, and why extreme events can dominate aggregate loss patterns. The book provides an integrated analysis of financial and operational vulnerabilities in the crypto market and DeFi platforms, with particular attention to fraud, exploits, and mechanisms that may undermine market integrity (OECD, 2022). The contribution is twofold. First, it offers a conceptual framing of how intermediation and trust are reconfigured in protocol-based environments and why this reconfiguration matters for risk formation and transmission. Second, it supports the discussion with empirical evidence drawn from historical incident data on DeFi exploits and illicit episodes, complemented by external reports and institutional sources, to identify salient patterns, concentrations, and emerging stress points.

The book is organized as follows. Chapter 1 establishes the conceptual foundation by examining how DeFi reconfigures financial intermediation and redistributes trust from centralized institutions to protocols and supporting infrastructures. Building on this reallocation of trust, Chap. 2 identifies the structural channels through which vulnerabilities arise, distinguishing between risks inherited from traditional finance and those amplified or generated by protocol design and governance mechanisms. Chap. 3 then situates these vulnerabilities within the concrete architecture of DeFi crypto-assets and organizational arrangements, including stablecoins, investment products, and multifunctional groups. Chap. 4 operationalizes the framework by introducing the methodological approach and presenting empirical evidence on incident frequency, loss magnitudes, and attack typologies across time and protocol segments. These empirical regularities inform Chap. 5, which proposes a refined taxonomy of DeFi risks grounded in observed patterns rather than purely conceptual classification. Chap. 6 extends the analysis to boundary infrastructures that mediate both resilience and illicit use, while Chap. 7 translates the findings into policy and stakeholder implications. Chapter 8 concludes by synthesizing the theoretical and empirical contributions and outlining directions for future research.

Overall, this book aims to clarify where fragility in DeFi originates and how it propagates, acknowledging the advancements while underscoring the operational, governance, and systemic challenges that emerge when financial intermediation is executed through protocols and DLTs.

References

Aramonte, S., Huang, W., & Schrimpf, A. (2021). DeFi risks and the decentralisation illusion. Bank for International Settlements. BIS Quarterly Review.

Bank of England. (2022). *Cryptoassets and decentralised finance: Financial stability in focus*. https://www.bankofengland.co.uk/financial-stability-in-focus/2022/march-2022

Committee on Payments and Market Infrastructures (CPMI) (2017). *Distributed ledger technology in payment, clearing and settlement: An analytical framework*. Bank for International Settlements.

European Systemic Risk Board (EBA–ESMA). (2025). *Crypto-assets and decentralised finance: Report on stablecoins, crypto-investment products and multi-function groups*. ESRB Cryptoasset Task Force.

Financial Stability Board (FSB). (2022). *Assessment of risks to financial stability from crypto-assets*. https://www.fsb.org/2022/02/assessment-of-risks-to-financial-stability-from-crypto-assets/

Financial Stability Board (FSB). (2023). *The financial stability risks of decentralised finance*. https://www.fsb.org/2023/02/the-financial-stability-risks-of-decentralised-finance/

International Monetary Fund. (IMF) (2025). *Understanding stablecoins. Monetary and Capital Markets Department*. https://www.imf.org/en/publications/departmental-papers/issues/2025/12/02/understanding-stablecoins-570602

International Monetary Fund-Financial Stability Board. (IMF-FSB) (2024). *G20 Cryptoasset Policy Implementation Roadmap, Status Report*. https://www.fsb.org/2024/10/g20-crypto-asset-policy-implementation-roadmap-status-report/

International Organization of Securities Commissions (IOSCO). (2023). *Policy recommendations for decentralized finance (DeFi)*.

Leo, S., & Panetta, I. C. (2023). *The Role of Distributed Ledger Technology in Banking: From Theory to Practice*. Cambridge University Press.

Organisation for Economic Co-operation and Development (OECD). (2022). *Why decentralised finance (DeFi) matters and the policy implications*. OECD Publishing.

Contents

Chapter 1
Financial Intermediation and Trust in Defi

Abstract The rise of decentralized finance compels a reconsideration of the very foundations of financial intermediation. In conventional systems, trust is institutionalized-anchored in regulated entities, contractual enforceability, and supervisory oversight. DeFi, by contrast, embeds trust within code, governance arrangements, and infrastructural components such as oracles and cross-chain bridges. This relocation does not signify the disappearance of intermediation; rather, it signals its redistribution across technical and organizational layers. The chapter argues that this structural reconfiguration reshapes accountability and generates novel dependencies, which in turn condition the specific vulnerabilities examined in subsequent chapters.

1.1 Financial Intermediation and Trust: From Institutions to Protocols

Traditional finance organises financial intermediation around legally recognised institutions (i.e., banks, insurance companies, brokers, exchanges and others) framing intermediation as an institutionalised process embedded within a system of rights, duties, and enforceable accountability. Within this institutional framework, intermediaries perform core financial functions, including the screening and monitoring of borrowers, the custody of assets, the provision of liquidity through market-making activities, the execution and settlement of transactions, the allocation of capital, and the transfer and pooling of risk. These functions are all carried out within a formal governance architecture that subjects institutions to prudential supervision, capital and liquidity requirements, internal control mechanisms, compliance obligations, and conduct-of-business standards. This layered regulatory environment is designed to mitigate information asymmetries and agency conflicts, align incentives between principals and agents, and contain systemic externalities internalising risks that would otherwise be dispersed across market participants or the broader financial system.

This prevailing institutional architecture began to be challenged by the emergence of DLT technologies, and in particular by blockchain architectures that demonstrated how transaction ordering and settlement could be achieved in open networks

L. Barbaro et al., *Crypto and Decentralized Finance Under Stress*,
SpringerBriefs in Finance, https://doi.org/10.1007/978-3-032-28425-9_1

through cryptographic verification and consensus[1] rather than through a single trusted operator. The advent of Bitcoin has introduced a new peer-to-peer network design aimed at reducing reliance on financial intermediaries for transaction validation and preventing double spending, i.e., the reuse of the same digital unit in multiple transactions. Building on this innovation, the idea of smart contracts, first conceptualised as "computerised transaction protocols" that can execute contractual clauses, provided a conceptual bridge from digital payments to programmable financial logic (Szabo, 1996). The launch of general-purpose smart contract platforms, most notably Ethereum, made it possible to encode more complex financial functions directly on-chain, enabling applications of automated exchange, collateralised lending, and protocol interactions. Institutional analyses have since discussed DLTs as a potential redesign of payment, clearing, and settlement arrangements highlighting both opportunities and new risk and governance questions when key functions are shifted from organisations to shared infrastructures (CPMI, 2017).

DeFi reconfigures this architecture by shifting parts of intermediation from institutions to protocols. In other words, instead of relying on organisational hierarchies and regulatory supervision, DeFi relies on (i) smart contracts that encode rules for transactions and state updates; (ii) crypto-economic incentives that coordinate behaviour; and (iii) modular infrastructures (e.g., oracles, bridges, custody solutions, front-ends) that connect protocol logic to market reality. Therefore, "disintermediation" is often better understood as "re-intermediation". In fact, intermediating functions do not disappear, they are decomposed and redistributed across code, governance, and infrastructure providers (Castillo León & Lehar, 2026). For instance, market making is implemented through Automated Market Maker (AMM) designs, credit allocation is frequently implemented through collateral rules and liquidation mechanisms, and settlement is anchored in blockchain consensus rather than institutional clearing and settlement systems. This shift deeply affects the notion of accountability. For instance, in TradFi, failures can be addressed through ex post enforcement against identifiable entities, through supervision, contractual remedies, or liability regimes. In DeFi, failures may be harder to remediate because the relevant "decision makers" can be dispersed (DAO governance), pseudonymous, or external to the protocol (e.g., oracle operators or bridge validators). Therefore, to understand DeFi, it is essential to characterise how intermediation is structured and where its critical dependencies lie.

[1] *Consensus* refers to the protocol-level mechanism by which a distributed network agrees on the valid order of transactions and the current ledger state without relying on a single central administrator.

1.2 The Reconfiguration of Trust in Decentralized Finance

Trust in financial systems generally concerns the reliability of counterparties, the integrity of transaction execution, the stability of infrastructures, and the enforceability of rules. In institution-based systems, trust is supported by legal frameworks, supervision, reputational constraints, and institutional risk management. In DeFi, by contrast, trust is reconfigured along different dimensions (IOSCO, 2023). First, trust shifts from institutional discretion to rule-based execution. Smart contracts can enable predictable execution. Thus, if correctly specified and implemented, they reduce certain forms of discretionary behaviour and operational opacity since the source code is accessible and verifiable from any of the contractors. This trust in code, however, is conditional (Atzei et al., 2017). It presumes that the code is correct, that assumptions are valid under stress, and that the supporting infrastructure (e.g., blockchain security, oracle feeds) behaves as expected. Code-based execution can therefore replace some agency problems but introduce new ones, such as software vulnerabilities, design flaws, and correlated failure modes.

Additionally, trust becomes sensitive to governance and upgradeability. Many protocols evolve through upgrades, parameter changes, and governance decisions. This means that users must trust the current code and the processes that can change with it. Who participates in the consensus mechanism, who votes, how quickly vulnerabilities are addressed, and whether emergency powers exist (and how they are protected) are all factors to take into account. Even in systems labelled "decentralized," governance power can be concentrated through token holdings, delegation structures, or privileged roles,[2] creating forms of "hidden centralization" that matter for both resilience and abuse. Furthermore, trust depends on boundary infrastructures that connect protocols to the external environment. For instance, among others, oracles[3] translate market information into on-chain state, bridges connect liquidity and assets across chains, front ends mediate user access, custody tools and wallets secure private keys, and privacy infrastructures affect traceability and enforcement. These components are often less visible than the core protocol but can become critical points of failure or exploitation. Importantly, users may not clearly distinguish between protocol risk and infrastructure risk, even though the operational consequences can be similar (Zetzsche et al., 2020). Finally, trust is

---

[2] DLT/Blockchain governance models can be described along two dimensions: visibility (public vs private) and consensus participation (permissionless vs permissioned). A public network is broadly accessible and its ledger is generally observable, whereas a private network restricts access and ledger visibility to a defined group of users. A permissionless network allows open participation in transaction submission and/or validation according to protocol rules, while a permissioned network restricts validation and ledger-writing to authorised entities.

[3] Oracles are systems or services that provide smart contracts with data external to the blockchain (off-chain data), such as market prices, exchange rates, or event outcomes. Because blockchain cannot autonomously access external information, oracles act as a bridge between the digital and real worlds, ensuring data reliability through cryptographic mechanisms or decentralized networks of validators.

shaped by market design and incentives. DeFi protocols frequently rely on incentive mechanisms (liquidity mining, governance tokens, fee sharing, staking rewards) to bootstrap participation. While incentives can promote growth and liquidity, they can also attract opportunistic behaviour, accelerate risk-taking, and create reflexive feedback loops, especially during bull markets. Trust can therefore be fragile and pro-cyclical, increasing during expansion phases and collapsing when expectations shift.

Taken together, these dimensions suggest that DeFi replaces some TradFi trust mechanisms with a composite form of trust that combines technical assurance, governance legitimacy, infrastructure reliability, and incentive compatibility. This composite trust can be powerful in normal conditions, but it can also be vulnerable to stress, coordination failures, and tail events. Code does not eliminate trust; it redistributes it across developers, governance token holders, infrastructure providers, and external data feeds. The next section builds on this point by explaining how protocol-based intermediation reorganises financial functions across code, governance, and supporting infrastructures.

1.3 Protocol-Based Intermediation as Organisational Logic

The transition from institution-based to protocol-based intermediation reconfigures the underlying architecture of the financial system. In traditional finance, the operation of markets relies on organisational routines, discretionary judgement, and supervisory oversight, with legal accountability functioning as an ex-post mechanism of enforcement and risk containment. The institutional form is therefore central to the production and enforcement of financial rules. By contrast, decentralised finance restructures intermediation around software-based procedures embedded in executable code. Participants interact through smart contracts deployed on shared ledgers, where transaction rules are predefined and automatically enforced by protocol logic rather than by managerial discretion or regulatory intervention. What would traditionally be understood as a financial institution is decomposed into a layered technological configuration in which protocol design, governance mechanisms, and ancillary service interfaces collectively perform exchange, credit, custody, and settlement functions (Werbach, 2018). In this setting, institutional authority is partially displaced by computational execution, and coordination emerges from interoperable modules rather than from vertically integrated organisational entities.

A defining trait of this model is its preference for ex-ante specification over ex-post discretion. Key conditions (e.g. collateral thresholds, liquidation triggers, fee rules, or priority logic) are written into contracts and executed automatically once the relevant state is observed. In normal conditions, this can increase predictability and verifiability since users can inspect the rule-set and observe state changes on-chain. Yet, when market conditions move outside the designers' assumptions, adjustment tends to occur through the mechanisms that the system already contains (e.g. parameter changes, upgrades, governance votes, or emergency procedures) rather than through real-time discretionary interventions. This matters because the range of possible responses is shaped by design. While automation reduces some forms of opacity and agency frictions, it also limits how quickly and in what ways the system can adapt. Furthermore, DeFi coordinates behaviour through crypto-economic design. Fees, rewards, penalties, collateral constraints, and issuance schedules are not merely technical parameters. They embody behavioural assumptions and shape strategic interaction among heterogeneous actors. Liquidity provision can be induced through fee revenues and token incentives and borrowing conditions can be governed by collateral ratios, liquidation penalties, and interest-rate curves. As the ecosystem matures, specialised participants (e.g. arbitrageurs, liquidators, and automated agents) learn to respond to these incentives at scale. Therefore, the performance of protocol-based intermediation depends on code correctness, but also on whether the incentive structure remains robust when participants optimise aggressively and when conditions change abruptly.

Furthermore, DeFi expands through modularity and composability. Protocols are often built as building blocks that plug into one another via shared standards and external services, enabling rapid innovation and interoperability (Schär, 2021). This architecture makes it possible to assemble new financial products without vertically integrating all functions inside a single organisation. At the same time, it distributes intermediation across a network of dependencies like price feeds, liquidity conditions, bridges, and other components that are not managed by hierarchical oversight but by interfaces and shared conventions. Authority and accountability are therefore reconfigured. Even when governance is presented as decentralised, practical control can be exercised through upgrade processes, delegation structures, and privileged roles at the protocol or infrastructure layer. Understanding who can change parameters, deploy upgrades, or influence critical dependencies becomes necessary for interpreting how protocol-based financial systems evolve and how they behave under stress.

References

Atzei, N., Bartoletti, M., & Cimoli, T. (2017). A survey of attacks on Ethereum smart contracts (SoK). In *Principles of Security and Trust* (POST 2017). Springer.

Castillo León, J., & Lehar, A. (2026). What data has told us about decentralized finance. *Journal of Corporate Finance, 96*. Article 102916.

Committee on Payments and Market Infrastructures (CPMI). (2017). *Distributed ledger technology in payment, clearing and settlement: An analytical framework*. Bank for International Settlements.

International Organization of Securities Commissions (IOSCO). (2023). *Policy recommendations for decentralized finance (DeFi).*

Szabo, N. (1996). Smart contracts: Building blocks for digital markets. *Extropy*, 16.

Schär, F. (2021). *Decentralized finance: On blockchain—And smart contract-based financial markets*. FRB of St. Louis Review. Available at SSRN: https://ssrn.com/abstract=3843844

Werbach, K. (2018). *The blockchain and the new architecture of trust*. MIT Press.

Zetzsche, D. A., Arner, D. W., Buckley, R. P., & Föhr, L. (2020). Decentralized finance. *Journal of Financial Regulation, 6*(2), 172–203.

Chapter 2
Traditional and Specific Risks of DeFi

Abstract A meaningful assessment of decentralized finance requires distinguishing between inherited financial risks and those emerging from its architectural particularities. Market volatility, liquidity mismatches, and credit exposure persist, yet they operate within a markedly different institutional environment. Smart contracts, token-based governance, composability across protocols, and infrastructural interconnections introduce new channels through which fragility may arise and propagate. This chapter develops a structured reading of these risks, emphasizing how protocol design and systemic interlinkages alter both their manifestation and their transmission. The analysis establishes the conceptual scaffolding necessary for the empirical investigation that follows.

* * *

Recent studies agree that DeFi reproduces many risks of traditional finance but adds new ones or amplifies some due to the technological and governance peculiarities of the protocols (Makarov et al., 2022). IOSCO (2023) highlights how DeFi is the result of a widening of information asymmetries and the absence of regulated intermediaries. In the following, we define the main theoretical risks identified in DeFi.

Market and liquidity risks. High volatility in cryptoasset prices and potential market inefficiencies. The absence of traditional market makers and reliance on algorithmic or centralized stablecoins that can cause low liquidity or sudden order book drain-ups in times of financial stress. For example, sudden and large swings in collateral values of lending platforms can trigger cascading liquidations (Cong et al., 2022). Furthermore, the anonymous/pseudonymous nature of transactions reduces the disciplining effects of reputation, potentially incentivizing excessive risk-taking compared to traditional markets. Automated mechanisms such as Automated Market Makers (AMMs) provide ongoing liquidity, but can expose liquidity providers to impermanent losses[1] and other unique risks. If liquidity is concentrated in a few

[1] Impermanent Loss is a reduction in the return incurred by liquidity providers in the AMM protocols of decentralized finance. It occurs when the price ratio between assets deposited in a liquidity pool

L. Barbaro et al., *Crypto and Decentralized Finance Under Stress*,
SpringerBriefs in Finance, https://doi.org/10.1007/978-3-032-28425-9_2

pools, investors may have difficulty unwinding positions without impacting the asset price (Angeris et al., 2020).

Credit risk and leverage in DeFi are structured in ways that differ fundamentally from traditional lending. In the absence of counterparty credit assessment and borrower specific risk evaluation, DeFi lending protocols typically rely on overcollateralization as a primary risk-mitigation mechanism. While this design reduces exposure to unsecured default, it does not eliminate credit risk. Because protocols generally lack identity verification and ongoing credit monitoring, lending conditions cannot be tailored to the borrower's individual risk profile; instead, risk management is embedded in algorithmic parameters such as collateral ratios, liquidation thresholds, and penalty rules that operate automatically on chain (Chen et al., 2020). Leverage is further amplified through the extensive use of derivatives and yield-enhancing strategies. Borrowers may recursively leverage positions by borrowing assets against posted collateral in order to increase exposure, thereby subjecting themselves to automated margin calls when loan-to-value ratios breach predefined thresholds (Lehar et al., 2022). This mechanism introduces procyclical dynamics, as price declines can trigger forced liquidations that reinforce downward market pressure. In addition, the availability of flash loans (i.e., uncollateralised loans that must be repaid within a single transaction block) facilitates rapid arbitrage and can enhance market efficiency. However, the same instrument has been used to execute flash attacks that exploit protocol vulnerabilities and manipulate prices, thereby exposing structural weaknesses in smart contract design (Qin et al., 2021).

Technological and smart contract risks. Errors or bugs in smart contract code can introduce vulnerabilities that can be exploited by malicious actors. These operational-technological risks include known attacks such as re-entrancy (unexpected recursive recall of a contract function), price oracle manipulations, attacks due to weak access controls, or even logical bugs in lending functions. (Schär, 2021). For instance, the 2016 "*The DAO*" hack on Ethereum (≈$60 million stolen) was due to a re-entrancy flaw. Other well-known cases have exploited mathematical errors in collateralization calculations or poorly implemented mint/burn functions.[2] Such programming language vulnerabilities account for 20% of known incidents in DeFi, although on average with relatively small losses ($1.7 million per incident) (Werbach, 2018). In addition to code bugs, cyber risk also includes attacks on the underlying infrastructure (e.g., consensus exploits or DoS[3] attacks on the blockchain network) and

varies from the time of entry, resulting in an imbalance in the quantities held. The loss is called "impermanent" since it can cancel if prices return to their initial levels, but becomes effective when funds are withdrawn in the presence of permanent changes. It represents an endogenous risk component of AMM models, proportional to the relative volatility of assets.

[2] Mint and burn functions are two fundamental operations in managing token supply on blockchain. The mint function allows the creation of new tokens and their crediting to a specific address, thus increasing the circulating amount of the digital asset; the burn function, on the other hand, permanently destroys existing tokens, reducing their overall supply.

[3] DoS (Denial of Service) attacks are malicious actions aimed at rendering a computer system, network, or smart contract unavailable or broken, overloading it with requests or exploiting logical vulnerabilities to block its execution.

attacks on team cybersecurity (e.g., theft of private keys or protocol administrator credentials).

Risks of fraud, scams, and illicit conduct. The crypto ecosystem has seen a proliferation of fraudulent schemes, primarily targeting retail investors. A widespread phenomenon in DeFi is rug pulls, in which project developers raise funds (e.g., through token sales or liquidity pools) and then disappear with the collected funds, leaving investors with worthless tokens. Ponzi-type schemes disguised as yield farming opportunities accounted for about 23% of all documented incidents, although with relatively small average losses (Rekt Database, 2023). Another well-known form of illicit conduct risk is algorithmic front-running: operators with advanced technological capabilities (bots with preferential access to mempools) insert their own transactions immediately before or after significant operations observed in advance. For example, by anticipating a large order on a DEX and reselling immediately afterward at a profit (sandwich attack), they exploit the fact that blockchain transactions are publicly visible before finalization (Daian et al., 2019). These practices exploit market microstructure and resemble forms of market abuse, often referred to as MEV (Maximal Extractable Value), and degrade the fairness of trade execution. Such activities have enabled the extraction of significant value: in 2022 alone, MEV bots generated at least $307 million in revenue on Ethereum, of which approximately $128 million came from sandwich attacks (front-running of user swaps) (Sun, 2025).[4] Moreover, the lack of KYC/AML requirements in many pseudonymous DeFi protocols facilitates illicit activities such as money laundering, often via DEXs and mixers. In 2021, more than 50% of stolen crypto funds were moved through DeFi platforms (DEXs, bridges) to launder them, and around 25% through mixers[5] and similar strategies, while the use of centralized exchanges for cash-out fell below 15% (Savelyeva et al., 2022). More generally, information asymmetry and opacity foster fraud: retail investors often lack adequate information or expertise to assess complex projects and may fall victim to false promises (e.g., unrealistically guaranteed returns).

Governance risks and hidden centralization. Many DeFi protocols have opaque or concentrated governance structures. DAOs (Decentralized Autonomous Organizations) that manage some protocols may have pseudonymous participation, but decision-making power is often concentrated in the hands of a few institutional investors or founding teams, through the possession of high stocks of governance tokens. This introduces conflicts of interest and the possibility of collusion, as well as the risk of decisions that are not transparent to the community. Moreover, decision making processes are very often slow since all members must vote this may cause operational inefficiencies and delays in addressing urgent vulnerabilities. A peculiar example of this risk is the possibility of so-called governance attacks. If

---

[4] *"Crypto Crime Trends for 2022: Illicit Transaction Activity Reaches All-Time High in Value, All-Time Low in Share of All Cryptocurrency Activity"* on Chainanalysis https://www.chainalysis.com/.

[5] Mixers (or cryptocurrency tumblers) are protocols or services that anonymize transactions on the blockchain by fragmenting and mixing the inputs and outputs of different users, making the origin of the funds untraceable. They work based on cryptographic aggregation and redistribution mechanisms, sometimes managed through smart contracts or decentralized networks.

an attacker accumulated enough voting tokens (for example, borrowing them with a flash loan), they could help pass malicious proposals (i.e., transfer protocol reserves). Finally, some protocols retain administrative keys (admin keys) or super-user privileges that allow maintainers to update contracts or stop the protocol in an emergency. If compromised, these keys could provide a hacker with complete control over the funds, as has happened in various Private Key Compromise exploits,[6] one of the most common attack techniques. Such single control points are anomalies in an otherwise decentralized environment and pose a significant operational risk.

Interconnection and systemic risks. The composable ("*lego-like*") nature of DeFi means that protocols are tightly interdependent. For example, a DEX may rely on an external oracle to obtain cryptocurrency prices; similarly, a lending protocol may accept as collateral LP[7] tokens from a DEX or assets derived from staking (such as Lido's stETH[8]). These internal linkages within DeFi create complex and often opaque dependency chains: a failure or attack affecting one component can cascade across multiple protocols. A paradigmatic case was the collapse of the TerraUSD/Luna ecosystem in 2022, which triggered the crisis of the hedge fund Three Arrows Capital and the failure of several exposed centralized lenders (Celsius, Voyager, etc.). In on-chain DeFi, stablecoins act as systemic hubs (e.g., USDC/USDT are widely used as units of account and collateral); a solvency or confidence shock affecting a major stablecoin could generate widespread contagion effects across the entire ecosystem. According to the FSB, the internal interconnectedness of cryptofinance and its structural interdependencies amplify the sector's intrinsic risks and could, in the future, transmit shocks to traditional finance if DeFi were to continue growing and integrating[9] At present, the direct exposure of banks and traditional financial intermediaries to cryptoassets remains limited; therefore, even during major shocks (such as those in 2022), contagion to the traditional financial system has remained relatively contained (Akartuna et al., 2022). However, this situation could change with the entry of institutional investors and the potential tokenization of traditional assets

[6] Private Key Compromise occurs when a private key (i.e. cryptographic element essential for authenticating and signing transactions on the blockchain) is stolen, exposed, or used by unauthorized parties. Since possession of the private key is equivalent to effective control of the associated digital assets, its compromise results in the irreversible loss of funds and the violation of the integrity of the wallet or protocol. The most common causes include phishing attacks, malware, vulnerabilities in custody systems, or poor credential management by the user. In the institutional setting, key compromise risk mitigation occurs using multi-signature custody solutions (multisigs), hardware wallets, and cryptographically isolated security models (hardware security modules—HSMs).

[7] The Liquidity Provider Token (LP token) is a digital asset that represents the share of liquidity deposited by a user in a liquidity pool of an AMM protocol. It serves as an on-chain receipt of contributed funds and accrued fees, allowing the holder to redeem their stake or use the token as collateral in other DeFi transactions.

[8] Lido stETH is a derivative token issued by the protocol "Lido Finance", which represents the "liquid" version of Ether (ETH) staked on the Ethereum network. When a user deposits ETH on Lido, they receive stETH tokens in exchange at a 1:1 ratio, which reflect the value of the deposit and accrue the returns generated by staking over time.

[9] "*Crypto Money Laundering Activity Spread Across More Service Deposit Addresses in 2023, Plus New Tactics from Lazarus Group*" on Chainanalysis https://www.chainalysis.com/.

on public blockchains. An additional aspect to consider is the risk of "cryptoization" of emerging economies: the widespread adoption of cryptoassets as substitutes for local currency (in contexts of high inflation or capital controls) could weaken the effectiveness of monetary policy and amplify financial vulnerabilities in those countries (Europol, 2023).

References

Akartuna, E.A., Johnson, S.D., & Thornton, A. (2022). Preventing the money laundering and terrorist financing risks of emerging technologies: An international policy Delphi study. *Technological Forecasting and Social Change, 179*, 121632.

Angeris, G., & Chitra, T. (2020). *Improved price oracles: Constant function market makers*. https://arxiv.org/abs/2003.10001

Chen, Y., & Bellavitis, C. (2020). Blockchain disruption and decentralized finance: The rise of decentralized business models. *Journal of Business Venturing Insights, 13*, Article e00151.

Cong, L. W., Li, Y., & Wang, N. (2022). Token-based platform finance. *Journal of Financial Economics, 144*(3), 972–991.

Daian, P., Goldfeder, S., Bentov, I., Kell, T., Breidenbach, L., Li, Y., Zhao, X., & Juels, A. (2019). *Flash boys 2.0: Frontrunning, transaction reordering, and consensus instability in decentralized exchanges*. https://arxiv.org/abs/1904.05234

International Organization of Securities Commissions (IOSCO). (2023). *Policy recommendations for decentralized finance (DeFi)*.

Lehar, A., & Parlour, C. A. (2022). *Systemic fragility in decentralised markets*. BIS working papers no. 1062. Bank for International Settlements.

Makarov, I., & Schoar, A. (2022). *Cryptocurrencies and decentralized finance (DeFi)*. NBER working paper no. 30006. National Bureau of Economic Research. https://www.nber.org/papers/w30006

Qin, K., Lazzaretti, L., Zhou, L., Gervais, A., & Afonin, Y. (2021). *CeFi vs. DeFi: Comparing centralized to decentralized finance*. https://arxiv.org/abs/2106.08157

Savelyeva, T., & Park, J. (2022). Blockchain technology for sustainable education. *British Journal of Educational Technology, 53*, 1591–1604. https://doi.org/10.1111/bjet.13273

Schär, F. (2021). *Decentralized finance: On blockchain- and smart contract-based financial markets*. FRB of St. Louis Review. Available at SSRN: https://ssrn.com/abstract=3843844

Sun, D., Ma, W., Nie, L., & Liu, Y. (2025). SoK: A taxonomic analysis of DeFi rug pulls: Types, dataset, and tool assessment. *Proceedings of the ACM on Software Engineering*.

Werbach, K. (2018). *The blockchain and the new architecture of trust*. MIT Press.

Chapter 3
DeFi Crypto Assets: Stablecoins, Crypto Asset Investment Products, and Multifunctional Groups

Abstract Within the broader DeFi ecosystem, asset typologies and organizational configurations exhibit heterogeneous risk profiles. Stablecoins, often presented as anchors of stability, raise fundamental questions concerning reserve composition, transparency, and regulatory arbitrage across jurisdictions. Crypto-asset investment products (CIPs) reveal the increasing entanglement between decentralized infrastructures and traditional financial intermediaries, particularly in custody and asset management functions. Multifunctional groups (MFGs), operating across multiple verticals of the crypto market, concentrate operational, governance, and cross-border risks in potentially systemic ways. Through comparative examination, this chapter situates these actors within the evolving architecture of decentralized intermediation.

* * *

Recently, the European Systemic Risk Board (ESRB) conducted an in-depth analysis of three key issues in the evolution of cryptoassets: stablecoins, crypto asset investment products (CIPs), and multifunctional groups (MFGs). These three areas reflect one of the main dynamics of the crypto ecosystem (ESRB, 2025).

3.1 Stablecoins

Stablecoins are cryptoassets designed to maintain a stable value against a reference, usually a single official currency such as the US dollar or the euro. Their defining feature is the attempt to combine the technological infrastructure of cryptoassets (i.e., programmability, peer-to-peer transferability, and operation on distributed ledgers) with a relatively stable nominal value. In economic terms, they resemble privately issued monetary claims holders expect to redeem them at par in the reference currency, and their acceptance depends on confidence in that promise. Stability is therefore not inherent in the token itself but derives from institutional arrangements. It depends on the composition and liquidity of reserve assets, the legal enforceability of

L. Barbaro et al., *Crypto and Decentralized Finance Under Stress*,
SpringerBriefs in Finance, https://doi.org/10.1007/978-3-032-28425-9_3

redemption rights, the operational robustness of issuance and custody mechanisms, and the credibility of disclosure and oversight (IMF, 2025; ESRB, 2025).

Different stabilisation mechanisms generate different risk structures. The dominant category consists of reserve-backed stablecoins. In these arrangements, the issuer holds off-chain assets (e.g. bank deposits, short-term sovereign securities, or money market instruments) intended to back the tokens in circulation. Trust in the stablecoin is mediated by legal claims on these reserves and by attestations or audits rather than by on-chain collateral verification. Other models rely on on-chain collateral, locking cryptoassets or tokenised financial instruments in smart contracts to support issuance. In such cases, stability is linked to the market value of collateral and to the integrity of price oracles and liquidation mechanisms. Algorithmic designs, which attempt to stabilise value through endogenous supply adjustments or incentive schemes, rely on expectations about market behaviour and can be particularly vulnerable to sudden regime shifts. The European regulatory framework (MiCAR) reflects these distinctions by classifying single currency tokens as e-money tokens (EMTs) and broader asset-linked arrangements as asset referenced tokens (ARTs), with corresponding regulatory obligations (ECB, 2025; ESRB, 2025). The technical architecture of a stablecoin is thus inseparable from its legal and prudential treatment.

In terms of scale, stablecoins have grown rapidly and are highly concentrated. By September 2025, global market capitalisation was around USD 300 billion, representing roughly 7.5% of the overall cryptoasset market. Almost the entire market is denominated in US dollars, and two issuers (USDT and USDC) account for most of the outstanding supply (ESRB, 2025).

The economic function of stablecoins today is primarily internal to the crypto ecosystem. They serve as settlement assets on trading platforms, as collateral in derivatives markets, and as a unit of account in DeFi. By providing a relatively stable reference point in an environment characterised by high volatility, they facilitate leverage, margining, and liquidity provision. In decentralised exchanges and lending protocols, stablecoins are routinely paired with more volatile tokens, allowing participants to manage short-term price risk without exiting the crypto environment. This infrastructure role explains why stablecoins are central to crypto-market microstructure even if their use in retail commerce remains modest. Evidence on real-economy payment use confirms this limited external usage. International monitoring indicates that most stablecoin transactions relate to trading or internal transfers within crypto platforms rather than to purchases of goods and services (IMF–FSB, 2024). External reports referenced in institutional assessments suggest that stablecoins account for a very small share of global e-commerce transactions and that central banks generally view their domestic use as marginal and concentrated in remittances or niche applications (ESRB, 2025). Stablecoins are therefore better described as a scalable private settlement layer for digital-asset markets than as a general-purpose payment instrument.

The main financial vulnerability of stablecoins is run risk. Because holders expect redemption at par, confidence plays a central role. If doubts arise about reserve adequacy, liquidity, or legal enforceability, redemption requests can rapidly increase.

In reserve-backed models, this may force issuers to liquidate assets quickly, potentially at a discount. Depegging episodes (i.e. situations in which the market price of a stablecoin deviates materially from its reference value) demonstrate how rapidly confidence can deteriorate. When a stablecoin is widely used as collateral, price instability can cascade into other markets. Liquidations in decentralised protocols can amplify downward pressure, while substitution into alternative stablecoins may produce opposite price movements. Such dynamics resemble classic liquidity spirals observed in traditional financial markets, albeit within a technologically distinct environment (ESRB, 2025; IMF, 2025).

Operational and governance risks compound these financial vulnerabilities. In facts, stablecoin stability relies on the integrity of custodians, payment rails, smart contracts, and blockchain networks. Cyber incidents, outages, or failures in redemption processes can undermine confidence even if reserves are adequate. Moreover, the broader crypto-technical stack (e.g., bridges and oracles) introduces additional points of fragility. Institutional assessments classify operational resilience and cyber risk alongside financial stability concerns (ESRB, 2025). Stablecoins also pose challenges in the areas of financial integrity and legal certainty. Their pseudonymous transferability and cross-border reach can facilitate illicit finance if AML/CFT controls are weak or unevenly applied. At the same time, regulatory fragmentation complicates enforcement. Differences in national regimes regarding custody, insolvency treatment, and redemption rights can create uncertainty about holders' legal position in stress scenarios (IMF-FSB, 2024; IMF, 2025). For a money-like instrument, such uncertainty directly affects credibility. Effective regulation must therefore address not only reserve quality but also governance, transparency, and enforceable legal claims.

Regulatory responses have increasingly adopted a risk-based approach. International bodies emphasise the need for high-quality, liquid reserves, segregation of assets, clear and timely redemption rights, and credible recovery and resolution frameworks for arrangements that could become systemic (IMF, 2025). The objective is to align stablecoin oversight with the risks they generate, rather than to treat them as purely technological innovations. The G20 monitoring framework acknowledges that real-economy use remains limited but stresses that interconnections with mainstream finance may deepen (IMF-FSB, 2024).

Looking ahead, the relevance of stablecoins depends less on their current payment share and more on their potential scale and integration. Projections of market growth vary widely, reflecting regulatory uncertainty and evolving use cases (IMF, 2025). At present, stablecoins remain primarily instruments of crypto-market settlement rather than general money substitutes. However, if reserve portfolios continue to expand and cross-border usage intensifies, their macrofinancial relevance could strongly increase. In that scenario, vulnerabilities linked to runs, reserve-market spillovers, operational fragility, and legal fragmentation would become more significant.

3.2 Crypto Asset Investment Products (CIPs)

Crypto Asset Investment Products (CIPs) are financial instruments designed to provide investors with exposure to cryptoassets without requiring direct ownership or technical management of the underlying tokens. Rather than holding private keys or interacting with blockchain protocols, investors access crypto markets through regulated vehicles structured under conventional financial law. In this sense, CIPs represent a process of financial intermediation and "securitisation" of crypto exposure, translating digitally native assets into formats compatible with traditional portfolio management and market infrastructures.

CIPs encompass a range of structures. They include exchange-traded products (ETPs), such as exchange-traded funds and exchange-traded notes referencing spot or derivative-based crypto exposures; open-ended and closed-end investment funds; index-tracking vehicles; structured notes and certificates; and other collective investment schemes with substantial cryptoasset allocations. Some CIPs incorporate leverage or derivative overlays to amplify exposure.

It is analytically useful to distinguish CIPs from two adjacent categories. The first consists of crypto derivatives (i.e., futures, options, and swaps referencing cryptoassets) which transfer market risk through contractual payoffs and may entail margining obligations beyond the initial investment. The second comprises crypto-related services provided by financial institutions, such as custody, brokerage, asset management, and marketing of crypto-linked products. While these services do not necessarily involve balance-sheet exposure to cryptoassets, they generate operational, legal, and reputational risks that can transmit stress to the broader financial system.

The market for CIPs expanded markedly from early 2024 onward, following regulatory developments in the United States, including the approval by the U.S. Securities and Exchange Commission of spot Bitcoin exchange-traded products. This decision catalysed both retail and institutional demand and encouraged established asset managers and financial intermediaries to enter the market. By July 31, 2025, global capitalisation of crypto asset investment products exceeded USD 235 billion, compared with approximately USD 130 billion in December 2024. Although still modest relative to global equity and bond markets, these volumes are no longer negligible from a macroprudential perspective. At least six individual CIPs had market valuations above USD 5 billion as of mid-2025. The three largest products alone reached capitalisations of approximately USD 85 billion, USD 24 billion, and USD 21 billion respectively, collectively accounting for nearly half of total market capitalisation (ESRB, 2025). This concentration implies that idiosyncratic events affecting a limited number of vehicles could have system-wide repercussions within the CIP segment.

Market infrastructure is similarly concentrated. The three largest custodial providers manage approximately 39% of all CIPs and account for 60% of total product capitalisation. Concentration is even more pronounced among physically backed products, where the same three custodians service at least 63% of vehicles and hold around 71% of overall capitalisation (ESRB, 2025). In some segments, roughly 80% of physically backed CIPs rely on a very small number of custodial entities. Most issuers of CIPs are located outside the European Union, while EU financial institutions currently play a comparatively limited direct role, though their involvement as service providers is increasing.

The growth of CIPs has coincided with a gradual but observable increase in participation by major traditional financial institutions, both as issuers and as custodians or service providers. Although overall activity remains contained relative to mainstream asset classes, this trend reflects a more permissive regulatory environment in certain jurisdictions and strengthens interconnections between crypto markets and traditional finance.

CIPs function by replicating, directly or indirectly, the price performance of one or more crypto assets. In physically backed structures, the issuer acquires and holds the underlying cryptoassets, typically through specialised custodians, and issues shares or units that represent a proportional claim on those holdings. Investors trade these shares on regulated exchanges or subscribe and redeem them according to fund rules, without direct interaction with blockchain infrastructure. In derivative-based or synthetic structures, exposure is achieved through futures, swaps, or other financial contracts referencing crypto assets. In these cases, the product's value derives from contractual payoffs rather than from ownership of the underlying tokens. Leverage may be embedded either structurally or through portfolio techniques, increasing sensitivity to price fluctuations.

From the investor's perspective, CIPs reduce operational barriers to entry. They eliminate the need to manage private keys, mitigate the risk of direct cyber theft, and integrate crypto exposure into conventional brokerage and custody accounts. From a systemic perspective, however, this intermediation transfers operational and custody risk from dispersed retail holders to centralised institutional actors. The integrity of private key storage, segregation of assets, and operational resilience of custodians becomes critical to market stability.

In the European Union, prudential treatment aims to constrain direct exposures of credit institutions. Since January 1, 2025, EU banks must apply a 1250% risk weight to cryptoasset exposures, effectively requiring more than the full capital backing. Two exceptions apply: exposures to tokenised traditional assets, including Electronic Money Tokens, are treated on a look-through basis; and exposures to MiCAR-compliant asset-referenced tokens referencing traditional assets carry a 250% risk weight. In addition, total exposures subject to the 1250% weight may not exceed 1% of a bank's Tier 1 capital. These measures limit direct balance-sheet risk but do not eliminate indirect exposures arising from sponsorship, custody, or derivative positions.

The risk profile of CIPs is multifaceted. Market risk is the most immediate dimension. First, ad widely acknowledged, cryptoassets are characterised by high price volatility, and sharp corrections can generate substantial losses for investors. While losses in most CIPs are capped at the invested amount, leveraged structures can amplify sensitivity to market swings. Second, concentration risk represents a structural vulnerability since the heavy reliance on a small number of custodians and service providers implies that operational failures, cyber incidents, or insolvency at a key intermediary could propagate rapidly across multiple products. Because physically backed CIPs depend on secure custody of private keys, disruptions at a dominant custodian could impair access to underlying assets, trigger valuation uncertainty, and undermine investor confidence. In extreme scenarios, contagion could extend beyond crypto markets if large traditional institutions are involved in custody or product sponsorship. Third, operational and cyber risks are accentuated by the technological characteristics of crypto markets. Hacks, fraud, and system outages occur with greater frequency than in conventional securities markets. Multifunctional groups (see Sect. 3.3) operating simultaneously as custodians and exchange platforms concentrate operational dependencies within single corporate structures. Failures in such entities could combine market, liquidity, and reputational shocks. Fourth, also counterparty and derivative risks deserve particular attention. Crypto derivatives can generate exposures exceeding initial investments and create margin call dynamics. Insolvency of key crypto market participants may lead to losses for financial institutions providing custody or derivative clearing services. Even where EU banks' direct exposures are limited by prudential rules, indirect channels, (e.g., non-bank financial institutions, fund holdings, or service provision) remain difficult to quantify. Finally, contagion risk is the overarching systemic concern. The expanding involvement of traditional financial institutions increases the potential for spillovers from crypto markets into the broader financial system. A large-scale disruption, such as the failure of a systemically important custodian or a run on a major stablecoin with multi-billion-dollar capitalisation, could transmit stress through asset liquidation channels, including markets for U.S. Treasury bills in which certain crypto-linked instruments invest. Institutions that issue stablecoins, sponsor CIPs, or provide critical infrastructure services could face liquidity or reputational pressures that impair their core intermediation functions. In extreme cases, public authorities might confront demands for emergency support to prevent disorderly market collapse.

In addition, data limitations complicate risk assessment. Significant gaps persist regarding leverage levels, derivative exposures, and the holdings of CIPs by non-bank financial institutions. Without comprehensive reporting, monitoring concentration and interconnectedness remains challenging. The persistent increase in market capitalisation and the clustering of infrastructure providers suggest that a threshold may be approaching at which localised disruptions generate broader systemic effects.

Overall, CIPs transform cryptoassets into instruments compatible with traditional financial portfolios, thereby lowering entry barriers and expanding market participation. Their growth, combined with concentrated service provision and increasing involvement of established financial institutions, creates new channels of interconnectedness between crypto markets and the conventional financial system. While current direct exposures in the euro area remain contained under stringent prudential treatment, continued expansion warrants close supervisory monitoring, enhanced data collection, and careful assessment of concentration, leverage, and operational resilience.

3.3 Multi-functions Groups

In assessing the implications of cryptoassets, attention should not be limited to the features of the tokens themselves, but also to the organisational structures. This section focuses on the entities that intermediate cryptoasset exposure and on the systemic implications of their growing involvement in this market.

Cryptoasset products and services in the EU can be offered by entities belonging to the same group as other financial and non-financial companies. Some of these groups can only operate in the crypto-business sector, while others can carry out a broad spectrum of financial or commercial activities. The term "multi-functional group" (MFG) is used to denote those groups offering different services related to crypto-activities within the EU.

Table 3.1 shows that MFGs engaged in crypto activities in the EU are classified into three main categories, based on their business models and regulatory status:

- Category 1, MFGs engaged exclusively in regulated crypto activities, such as the provision of crypto services or the issuance of crypto-activities.
- Category 2, MFGs performing both regulated cryptoasset activities and other financial services. This category is further divided into:
  (a) 2a MFGs primarily focused on the crypto sector.
  (b) 2b MFGs primarily involved in traditional finance, such as banking and payments.
- Category 3, which includes all other MFGs, including non-financial groups such as big tech.

Table 3.1 Classification of MFGs engaged in crypto activities in the European Union

Category	Core business	Role of crypto activities	Typical examples
MFG 1	Crypto only	Cryptoasset activities constitute the entire regulated business model	Crypto exchanges, custodians, issuers of EMTs
MFG 2a	Crypto-led with ancillary financial services	Crypto remains the main activity, while traditional financial services play a complementary role	Crypto firms also offering payments or limited financial intermediation
MFG 2b	Traditional finance with crypto exposure	Traditional financial services remain predominant, while crypto activities are carried out within part of the group	Banking groups, payment groups, or other regulated financial institutions with crypto-related entities
MFG 3	Non-financial commercial groups with crypto activities	The main business lies outside finance, but the group also performs regulated cryptoasset activities	Large corporates, including big tech groups

Source Author's elaboration based on ESRB CATF (2025)

Financial losses or reputational damage arising from crypto asset related activities may not remain confined to a single third-country entity but can affect the entire group structure. Many multifunctional groups (MFGs) operate across jurisdictions, often combining regulated and unregulated activities within the same corporate perimeter. Some maintain significant operations outside the European Union; others engage in cryptoasset activities that remain only partially regulated or entirely outside existing supervisory frameworks. In certain cases, MFGs are primarily active in jurisdictions where activities that fall within the scope of MiCAR in the EU are not yet subject to equivalent regulatory standards. Moreover, even within the EU, some groups participate in activities related to unregulated cryptoassets, including crypto lending, financing arrangements, or blockchain validation services.

From a microprudential perspective, the opportunities and risks associated with cryptoasset activities tend to be broadly comparable across different types of MFGs. However, the scale of operations, the degree of intra-group interdependence, the intensity of links with the broader crypto ecosystem, and the extent of connections with traditional financial institutions can magnify these risks. When sufficiently large and interconnected, such exposures may acquire macroprudential relevance. The capacity of MFGs to combine issuance, trading, custody, and related services within integrated platforms can foster innovation, reduce transaction costs, and enhance user accessibility. Economies of scale, unified infrastructure, and rapid product development allow these groups to respond efficiently to evolving market demand.

At the same time, these structural characteristics generate vulnerabilities. Financial interdependencies within the group, operational concentration, cyber risks, governance weaknesses, conflicts of interest, and reputational spillovers can be amplified by centralisation and cross-functional integration. Complex corporate structures and cross-border regulatory fragmentation further complicate effective supervision, particularly where parent entities are established outside the EU. These factors underscore the importance of assessing MFG configurations when evaluating systemic risk and determining whether existing regulatory and supervisory frameworks remain adequate. In the followings, we discuss the most recurring risk scenarios.

3.3.1 Intra-Group Financing and Liquidity Risks

Within-group financing difficulties, including liquidity problems, can generate risks for both MFGs and the broader market. MFGs, like other interconnected conglomerates, may depend on intra-group funding for their operations. Such dependencies can propagate risk within the group. For example, if a subsidiary experiences a significant outflow of funds, perhaps to meet claims under stressed market conditions, or to pay a penalty or compensation due to a serious operational or conduct breach (i.e., a data breach or sanctions), other group entities may need to step in to support its strength. Group entities could also suffer losses if the subsidiary fails to repay intra-group financing under the established terms. If such entities were to engage in relevant financial activities (for example, lending), any impairment of their operational capacity could generate broader risks to the system.

3.3.2 Operational and Technological Risks

MFGs can be particularly vulnerable to operational risks, particularly technological and information technology risks, due to their heavy dependence on common or interconnected technological infrastructures. If the MFG handles large transaction volumes or values, an operational disruption can generate systemic risks. The concentration of infrastructure can cause an interruption or breach in an area to impact a wide range of services, assuming macroprudential relevance. For example, if central systems such as authentication servers or trading platforms were compromised, attackers could gain widespread access to the systems, with ripple effects (such as severe disruptions to crypto markets) that would extend beyond the MFG itself. Furthermore, the greater the market share of the MFG, the more it becomes a target for malicious actors' intent on stealing data or crypto assets or extorting a ransom (as in the case of the Bybit exchange attack, see Annex 2). Such actors can be both external and internal. Human errors can also have amplified effects due to the scale of the group's operations.

3.3.3 Governance Risks, Conflicts of Interest and Reputation

MFGs' structure and business models can pose risks related to governance challenges and conflicts of interest, which can result in reputational damage with contagion effects towards other entities perceived as similar. The vertical and horizontal integration of multiple crypto asset-related issuance services and/or activities under a single umbrella, often characterized by opaque governance, increases the likelihood that such challenges and conflicts will emerge. Poor customer interactions can quickly erode trust in the MFG group. This can affect the group itself and also the stability of the broader crypto market, if other entities are perceived as having similar problems.

3.3.4 Effects of Contagion and Loss of Confidence

A loss of market confidence in an MFG can trigger contagion. Reputational damage can lead to sudden withdrawals from platforms operating in similar markets, forcing the forced sale of crypto assets. This could destabilize not only the affected group, but also the crypto assets, platforms or interconnected services, propagating the risk of contagion.

3.3.5 Concentration and Market Power Risks

A significant concentration of market power in an MFG can transform micro-prudential risks into macro-prudential risks. Centralization and concentration can create systemic vulnerabilities and increase the potential for market manipulation. For example, Binance not only operates one of the largest crypto asset exchanges in the world, but also controls the Binance Smart Chain (BSC),[1] over which it exerts significant influence on network governance and validator selection. This vertical integration allows Binance to control different levels of the transactional process, raising concerns about market concentration and potential conflicts of interest. Globally, crypto asset markets show high levels of concentration, with few MFGs (non-banks) dominating trading volumes. The Herfindahl–Hirschman Index (HHI) indicates that the crypto asset market was "highly concentrated" in 2023 (HHI > 2500), with the market share of the five major exchanges steadily growing over the past five years. Recent analyses show that around 90% of trades are executed on the ten largest global exchanges, with Binance alone accounting for more than 50% of global trading volumes. The second largest exchange, UPbit, records only about a seventh of that volume. High levels of concentration are also observed within the EU, where 95% of transactions conducted on authorised CASPs in the EU are attributable to two platforms: Binance and Coinbase. Furthermore, Bitvavo and Kraken dominate the volume of euro-denominated exchanges. This concentration implies that any problems of such groups may have wider repercussions because of the scale of their operations. Similar concentration risks are also observed in the stablecoins market, with USDT issuer Tether Ltd representing a prime example of concentration risk, given its dominant role in providing liquidity—in addition to the wider risks arising from the lack of transparency on its reserves and the potential impact on market stability in the event of a loss of confidence in USDT (ESRB, 2025).

From a supervisory point of view, the multifunctional nature of many Category 1 and Category 2a MFGs generates structural challenges. These groups often combine cryptoasset-related activities within complex and, at times, opaque corporate structures. Such opacity may hinder supervisors in identifying the relevant competent authorities and in obtaining a clear, consolidated view of risk exposures across the group. In some cases, groups may structure their operations in a way that exploits regulatory differences across jurisdictions, establishing key entities in locations characterised by weaker oversight or by the absence of industry-specific regulation, as illustrated by the FTX[2] case. In the absence of effective ex-ante mechanisms ensuring

[1] The Binance Smart Chain (BSC) is a public blockchain developed by the Binance Group with the goal of providing a high-performance infrastructure for running decentralized applications (dApps) and smart contracts compatible with the Ethereum Virtual Machine (EVM).

[2] FTX was a major crypto-asset exchange group. In November 2022 it collapsed following liquidity stress and revelations of severe governance and internal-control failures, including weaknesses in record-keeping and the segregation of client assets, as well as opaque intra-group relationships. The case is widely cited as an example of how cross-border structuring and limited consolidated oversight can hinder supervisors in obtaining a clear view of group-wide exposures and responsibilities.

timely monitoring and mitigation, risks arising in less regulated parts of the group may propagate to other entities within the same structure.

Supervisory effectiveness is further constrained by the fact that most large Category 1 and Category 2 MFGs are constituted outside the European Union. This geographical dimension may limit the capacity of EU supervisors to exert effective oversight over activities that nonetheless affect EU investors and markets. The risk is amplified by the possibility for EU customers to interact with non-EU entities through reverse solicitation, namely where an EU client voluntarily approaches a service provider not established in the Union, without prior active marketing in the EU. Although ESMA Guidelines clarify that reverse solicitation must be interpreted restrictively and cannot serve as a mechanism to circumvent MiCAR requirements, its existence introduces potential gaps in regulatory compliance and consumer protection.

From a macroprudential perspective, the ability of authorities to identify and mitigate risks ex ante is weakened by the absence of consolidated group supervision frameworks for non-bank MFGs. Consolidated supervision arrangements are currently available only for banking groups and do not extend to other types of groups. The supervisory framework for financial conglomerates applies solely to certain combinations of traditional banking, insurance, and investment activities and predates the emergence of cryptoasset-related business models. MiCAR introduces supervisory colleges for significant asset-referenced tokens (ARTs) and significant electronic money tokens (EMTs), yet this framework focuses on specific issuance activities rather than on the broader range of cryptoasset services conducted within integrated groups. Although MiCAR provides for cooperation agreements between EU and third-country authorities, no formal and structured mechanism ensures systematic group-level cooperation with non-EU supervisors, despite the widespread presence of relevant groups outside the Union.

Although no systemic risk has yet been formally identified, National Competent Authorities (NCAs), together with the EBA and ESMA, should prioritise strengthening arrangements for group-wide supervisory dialogue concerning non-bank MFGs engaged in significant cryptoasset-related activities the EU. From a macroprudential standpoint, enhanced coordination and information-sharing would support more effective risk identification and mitigation. Should the size and value of cryptoasset-related exposures among non-bank MFGs in the EU increase significantly, the regulatory framework may require further enhancement to introduce more formal provisions ensuring group-wide reporting and to facilitate effective supervisory dialogue, including structured cooperation with third-country authorities (ESRB, 2025).

References

European Systemic Risk Board (EBA–ESMA). (2025). *Crypto-assets and decentralised finance: Report on stablecoins, crypto-investment products and multi-function groups*. ESRB Cryptoasset Task Force.

International Monetary Fund-Financial Stability Board (IMF-FSB). (2024). *G20 cryptoasset policy implementation roadmap, status report*. https://www.fsb.org/2024/10/g20-crypto-asset-policy-implementation-roadmap-status-report/

International Monetary Fund (IMF). (2025). *Understanding stablecoins*. Monetary and Capital Markets Department. https://www.imf.org/en/publications/departmental-papers/issues/2025/12/02/understanding-stablecoins-570602

Chapter 4
DeFi Under Stress: Statistics on Fraudulent Events

Abstract The analytical framework developed thus far finds empirical grounding in a structured dataset of DeFi-related security incidents covering the period 2016–2025. This chapter details the methodological choices underpinning the dataset, including source triangulation, classification criteria, and definitional boundaries. Total Value Locked (TVL) is employed as an indicative measure of ecosystem scale, allowing loss magnitudes to be contextualized within broader market dynamics. The empirical results point to a pronounced concentration of losses in high-impact events, recurring technical vectors, and significant cross-chain spillovers. These patterns suggest that observed incidents are not episodic anomalies, but reflections of deeper structural characteristics.

* * *

4.1 Data and Sample

In this section, we present an analysis on the incidents data (e.g., hacker attacks, fraud, exploits and others) that occurred within the DeFi ecosystem between 2016 and 2025. The dataset we used for the analysis was obtained from DeFiLlama,[1] an open-access data platform that tracks and aggregates information on security incidents affecting DeFi protocols and related cryptoasset projects. Its "*Hacks*" section provides a database of exploit events, reporting key details including the affected protocol, date of occurrence, estimated financial losses, and a brief description of the attack vector. The platform compiles data from public disclosures, on-chain analysis, and community reporting, offering a reliable overview of the scale and typology of losses within the DeFi ecosystem. Although it does not constitute an official or regulatory source, it is widely employed for analytical purposes due to its breadth of coverage and real time updating of incident statistics. The dataset is complemented

[1] DeFiLlama platform and data are available at: https://defillama.com/hacks.

L. Barbaro et al., *Crypto and Decentralized Finance Under Stress*,
SpringerBriefs in Finance, https://doi.org/10.1007/978-3-032-28425-9_4

by information drawn from threat intelligence and incident reports published by CertiK[2] (2024) and SlowMist[3] (2024).

Between 2016 and 2025, a total of 384 incidents are documented across multiple decentralized platforms, resulting in approximately \$11,699,499 million in misappropriated or lost assets. Each incident included in the dataset has been classified according to the attributes described in Table 4.1.

Considering the attributes described in Table 4.1, in the following sections, our analysis focuses specifically on the risk dimension, with particular attention to the incidents that have affected DeFi protocols. Each table reports a set of summary measures for each category (i.e., year, attack, blockchain platform, target, attack technique and fraud class). Incidents (N) represent the count of observed loss events in that category. Share of incidents (%) expresses how frequently the category occurs relative to the full sample. Total loss (USD mln) is the aggregate value of funds lost within the category, reported in millions of U.S. dollars. Share of total loss (%) indicates how much the category contributes to overall losses across the dataset. Finally, Avg loss per incident (USD mln) captures the typical severity of events in the category by reporting the average loss per incident, again in millions of U.S. dollars. For each table, we also provide the corresponding plot to visually support interpretation. Appendices A and B respectively provide the complete specification of the attack methods (including the respective definitions) and the list of blockchain platforms where the incidents occurred.

4.2 Market Growth and Fraudulent Events

The DeFi ecosystem began to take shape around 2017 and experienced rapid expansion from 2020 onward. This growth is captured by Total Value Locked (TVL), which measures the USD-denominated market value of cryptoassets deposited in DeFi smart contracts at a given point in time. TVL reflects both net capital inflows and fluctuations in underlying token prices. It therefore represents the actual economic exposure of the DeFi system instead of the cumulative investment flows. It becomes economically meaningful from 2020, although earlier observations are reported for completeness. Table 4.2 summarises the evolution of DeFi Total Value Locked (TVL) over 2016–2025, based on DeFiLlama data.

TVL is reported in million USD (USD mln) and can be read as end-of-year ("closing") values and annual averages ("mean"). The early figures remain negligible until 2018 and rise significantly in 2019, when end-of-year TVL reaches \$613.38 million. The sector's first major expansion begins in 2020, with TVL closing the year at \$15,067.39 million. This phase is consistent with the spread of yield-farming

[2] https://www.certik.com/.

[3] https://www.slowmist.com/.

Table 4.1 Incidents attributes

Attribute	Label	Description
Attack technique	Technique	The primary method used by attackers (e.g. Private Key Compromise, Flash Loan Attack, Reentrancy, phishing, etc.). In total, over 140 different attack or exploit techniques were identified, then grouped into more general categories for statistical analysis purposes
Type of fraud/ vulnerability	Classification	Taxonomy-based label identifying the primary nature of the incident (see Table 4.7), distinguishing between ecosystem-level failures, rug pulls, smart-contract or protocol vulnerabilities, and infrastructure-level attacks
Lost funds	LFund	The total assets lost or subtracted during the attack calculated at the time of the incident. The amount is expressed in dollars and indicates the financial severity of each DeFi incident
Blockchain	Chain	The blockchain on which the affected protocol operated at the time of the attack (Ethereum, BSC, Solana, etc.)
Target hit	Target	The type of target hit during the attack. It is used to distinguish where the breach occurred (DeFi protocol, exchange, bridge, DEX, CEX, etc.) and to identify risk patterns specific to the type of infrastructure. This data enables cross-chain and category-by-service DeFi analytics
Victim Entity	Name	It identifies the name of the entity that was a victim of the attack
Cross-chain bridge engagement	Bridge hack	A dummy variable that indicates whether the attack hit a cross-chain bridge, which is an infrastructure that allows the transfer of assets between different blockchains
Funds recovered	Amount returned	Amounts of funds recovered after the incident
Programming language	Language	Programming language used by the protocol
Date of incident	Date	The day the attack occurred or was made public
Source	Source	Source of the report (URL, bibliographic reference, etc.). It serves both to ensure data traceability and to assess the reliability of reporting

and liquidity-incentive programmes, whereby users deposit assets into protocols and receive token rewards that can confer governance rights or be traded on the market.[4]

The bull-cycle peak is clearly visible in 2021 where TVL closes at $163,281.96 million (+983.68% YoY). Notably, the annual mean increases accordingly to

[4] Report from CoinDesc at: https://www.coindesk.com/.

Table 4.2 End-of-year TVLs 2020–2025

Year	TVL closing (USD, mln)	TVL mean (USD, mln)	YoY change %	YoY mean %
2016	–	–	–	–
2017	–	–	–	–
2018	$3.93	$15.56	–	–
2019	$613.38	$436.38	15,507.63%	2704.50%
2020	$15,067.39	$4760.27	2356.45%	990.85%
2021	$163,281.96	$98,195.51	983.68%	1962.81%
2022	$38,465.48	$87,088.41	−76.44	−11.31%
2023	$52,850.95	$44,747.75	37.40%	−48.62%
2024	$116,183.53	$86,285.68	119.83%	92.83%
2025	$115,770.80	$121,692.85	0.36%	41.03%
Total	$ 502,237.42	$443,222.41	–	–

$98,195.51 million, indicating that the expansion was not confined to a year-end spike but reflected higher levels of locked value throughout the year.

The subsequent contraction is captured by the divergence between closing and mean values in 2022, as graphically illustrated in Fig. 4.1. While TVL closes 2022 at $38,465.48 million (−76.44% YoY), the annual mean remains high at $87,088.41 million (−11.31% YoY). This pattern suggests that a substantial portion of the decline materialised during the year (rather than being uniform throughout), consistent with the systemic shock and confidence loss triggered by events such as the UST/LUNA collapse in May 2022 (IOSCO, 2023). In 2023, TVL partially recovers in closing terms to $52,850.95 million (+37.40% YoY), but the annual mean falls to $44,747.75 million (−48.62% YoY), indicating that the average liquidity base across the year remained weaker than in 2022 despite the year-end rebound.

In 2024, both measures rebound: TVL closes at $116,183.53 million (+119.83% YoY) and the annual mean rises to $86,285.68 million (+92.83% YoY). Finally, 2025 shows stabilisation in end-of-year terms, with TVL closing at $115,770.80 million (+0.36% YoY). At the same time, the annual mean increases to $121,692.85 million (+41.03% YoY), implying that TVL was, on average, higher across 2025 than in 2024 even though it ended the year at a similar level, consistent with a more sustained activity regime rather than a purely year-end valuation effect.

Additionally, Fig. 4.1 illustrates the same dynamics by contrasting end-of-year TVL with the annual mean. Two aspects are particularly informative. First, the gap observed in 2022, with a high annual mean ($87,088.41 million) but a significantly lower year-end closing value ($38,465.48 million), suggests that the contraction was concentrated in the latter part of the year, consistent with a broader deleveraging phase after systemic stress in the crypto ecosystem (IOSCO, 2023). Second, in 2025 the pattern reverses: while the closing value is essentially flat versus 2024, the annual mean rises materially (USD 121.69 billion), indicating that TVL remained elevated for most of the year and that the end-of-year snapshot does not fully capture the

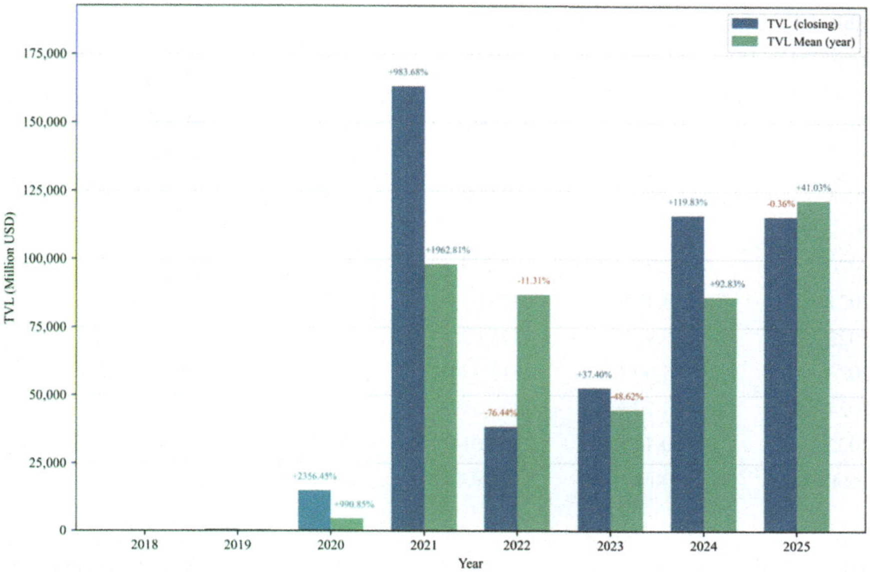

Fig. 4.1 Annual TVL: year-end versus annual average (USD mln), 2018–2025

average level of activity. Overall, the joint use of closing and mean TVL helps distinguish temporary year-end effects from changes in the underlying liquidity and collateral base supporting DeFi activity.

Another relevant driver behind the 2022 contraction was the liquidity crisis of algorithmic stablecoins. These *"stable"* cryptocurrencies were not backed by reserves but relied on equilibrium mechanisms that proved fragile under stress. As market confidence deteriorated, most notably following the UST/LUNA collapse, investors withdrew liquidity, amplifying deleveraging dynamics across DeFi (IOSCO, 2023). In 2023, the sector entered a consolidation phase. Despite a partial year-end recovery in closing TVL, the annual mean remained weaker, consistent with reduced retail risk appetite and a reallocation toward more robust protocols. In 2024, TVL rebounded strongly, supported by renewed market conditions and by the expansion of liquid staking and restaking activity, alongside the continued scaling of Ethereum Layer 2 infrastructures.[5] In 2025, end-of-year TVL remained broadly stable relative to 2024, while the annual mean increased, suggesting a more sustained level of activity throughout the year and a gradual shift toward a more mature market regime.

Even from the DeFiLlama dataset, we observe a growth in incidents within the expansion of the DeFi sector. Table 4.3 reports the number of incidents recorded per year with the corresponding total and average losses, in the period between 2016 and 2025.

A total of 384 incident cases were detected, for a total subtracted amount of $11,699,449 million and an overall average loss per incident of $30.467 million. In

---

[5] See https://www.coindesk.com/tag/cointelegraph.

Table 4.3 Number of incidents and total losses per year

Year	Incidents (N)	Share of incidents (%)	Total loss (USD mln)	Share of total loss (%)	Avg loss per incident (USD mln)
2016	1	0.26%	60.000	0.51%	60.000
2017	2	0.52%	157.700	1.35%	78.850
2018	2	0.52%	769.000	6.57%	384.500
2019	–	–	–	–	–
2020	16	4.17%	183.750	1.57%	11.484
2021	71	18.49%	2359.683	20.17%	33.235
2022	65	16.93%	3323.628	28.41%	51.133
2023	96	25.00%	1517.474	12.97%	15.807
2024	91	23.70%	1272.599	10.88%	13.985
2025	40	10.42%	2055.614	17.57%	51.390
Total	384	100%	11,699,449	100%	30.467

2019, Defillama's analysis reported no incidents. The results show that the two-year period 2021–2022 was a period of explosion of DeFi fraud and hacks, in parallel with the boom in the crypto market and the birth of thousands of new protocols. The number of known incidents went from a few cases per year before 2020, to 71 in 2021 and 65 in 2022, while the subtracted value rose from $184 million (2020) to $2359 million (2021) to a record $3323 million in 2022 (Chainalysis[6] report estimates ~ $3800 million in 2022, historical record).

In 2021, the DeFi Summer[7] wave saw the proliferation of protocols and yield farms, unfortunately accompanied by a wave of rug pulls and fraudulent schemes. As depicted in Fig. 4.2, The 2022 was marked by massive hacks against major DeFi protocols (Wormhole, Ronin, Beanstalk, Nomad, etc.) and the collapse of Terra/ Luna, events that explain the aggregate value subtracted. In 2023, the theft trend remained high in terms of the number of attacks (96 incidents in the dataset for 2023, up from 2022), but with lower average losses. This may indicate a fragmentation of attacks into many smaller events, or increased effectiveness of countermeasures that reduced the average amount per hack. Year 2024 shows an elevated number of incidents (91 cases, $1272 million lost), a sign that the threat remains real. In 2025, some of the largest thefts ever have already been recorded (e.g., Bybit 2025, $1.4 billion subtracted), bringing 2025 to over $2055 million in losses. It is therefore clear that, although 2022 remains the dark year for DeFi so far, the sector's vulnerability remains high, with potential new spikes linked to single major attacks.

---

[6] https://www.chainalysis.com/.

[7] The term DeFi Summer refers to the period, primarily between June and September 2020, when the decentralized finance ecosystem experienced explosive growth in terms of total value locked, number of protocols, and on-chain financial innovation. This phenomenon was triggered by the spread of liquidity mining and yield farming mechanisms, which incentivized users to provide liquidity in exchange for governance tokens and high returns.

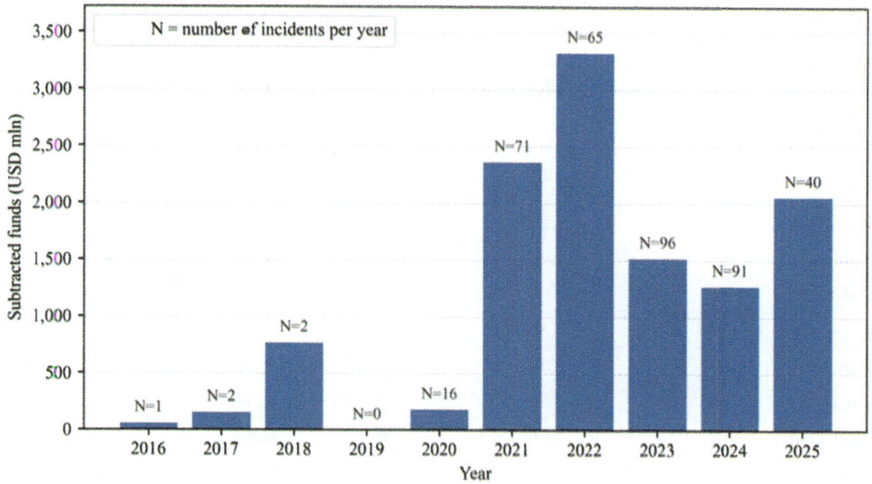

Fig. 4.2 Total losses per year

Analysing the phase of protocol life at which incidents occur, another interesting dynamic emerges: many attacks occur within a few months of the project's launch. Many DeFi protocols that emerged during the 2020–2021 boom quickly collapsed due to bugs or fraud. For example, AnubisDAO (2021), a fork of OlympusDAO, suffered a dramatic rugpull just 20 h after launch, with $60 million in ETH subtracted from the liquidity pool. In general, rugpulls tend to occur on very young projects (exit scams often occur as soon as the initial capital is raised), while hacks on more mature protocols can occur even after years of operation—for example, the BadgerDAO hack in 2021 hit a project launched in 2020, and in 2023 vulnerabilities in the Vyper scripting language caused exploits on Curve pools created years earlier. One potential summary metric is *Mean Time To Exploit*. It would likely show that many DeFi projects fail to *"pass the test of time"* without incident. This suggests the importance for investors to be wary of newborn protocols with amazing promises until they have built a security track record.

4.3 Blockchain and Target Segmentation

As far as blockchain platform and targets, Table 4.4 shows that Ethereum is the most affected platform in absolute value (it is the basis of larger DeFi protocols), but significant incidents occur on all major blockchains. In terms of the number of attacks, 48% of the incidents catalogued involved protocols on Ethereum, followed by Binance Smart Chain (11%), Arbitrum (7%), Solana (4%) and other ecosystems (Polygon, Avalanche, Fantom, etc.).

Table 4.4 Number of incidents and total losses per platforms

Platform	Incidents (N)	Share of incidents (%)	Total loss (USD mln)	Share of total loss (%)	Average loss per incident (USD mln)
Ethereum	184	47.92	7351.826	62.84	39.956
BSC	43	11.20	983.126	8.40	22.863
Arbitrum	28	7.29	76.253	0.65	2.723
Solana	15	3.91	555.495	4.75	37.033
Polygon	10	2.60	79.609	0.68	7.961
Avalanche	9	2.34	97.420	0.83	10.824
Base	9	2.34	35.785	0.31	3.976
Blast	6	1.56	71.750	0.61	11.958
Optimism	6	1.56	66.100	0.56	11.017
Fantom	6	1.56	61.313	0.52	10.219
Others	68	17.71	2320.771	19.84	34.129
Total	384	100.00	11,699.449	100.00	30.467

Considering the relative size of ecosystems, alternative chains exhibit proportionally less fraud and rugpulls (as evidenced by the overrepresentation of BSC in 2021–22 rugpulls) (Rekt Database, 2023), likely due to lower costs of launching scam tokens and lower scrutiny. Ethereum, while dominating in count, has a higher percentage of complex and high-profile attacks (e.g., hacks on blue chip protocols or infrastructures such as bridges connected to Ethereum). In 2022, 9 of the 10 largest hacks by value hit DeFi protocols, many of which were bridges or cross-chain hubs.[8] DEXs and decentralized trading platforms, on the other hand, experience a higher number of minor incidents (rugpulls of listed tokens, price manipulations on illiquid pools) but rarely individual events reach hundreds of millions of dollars in damage. A comparison of categories suggests that risk is often proportional to TVL. DeFi sectors with more capital (bridges, lending, stablecoins) attract more profitable attacks, while experimental or niche sectors (e.g., small yield aggregators, NFTfi protocols) see smaller incidents. Interestingly, some incidents also reflect interactions between different protocols. For instance, several price oracle manipulation attacks simultaneously involved a DEX (where the price of a low-liquid token is manipulated) and a lending platform (where the manipulated price is exploited to overborrow). This poses additional security challenges, because the attack surface extends across the boundaries of individual protocols (Fig. 4.3).

Overall, the evidence suggests that widespread and concentrated risks coexist on the one hand, many small *"daily"* frauds undermine market integrity and retail user trust, on the other, a few rare events threaten overall stability with significant losses and systemic propagation. This empirical evidence will guide the proposed

[8] TRM Labs: "*Traces Stolen Crypto from 2022 LastPass Breach*". Avaiable at: https://www.trmlabs.com.

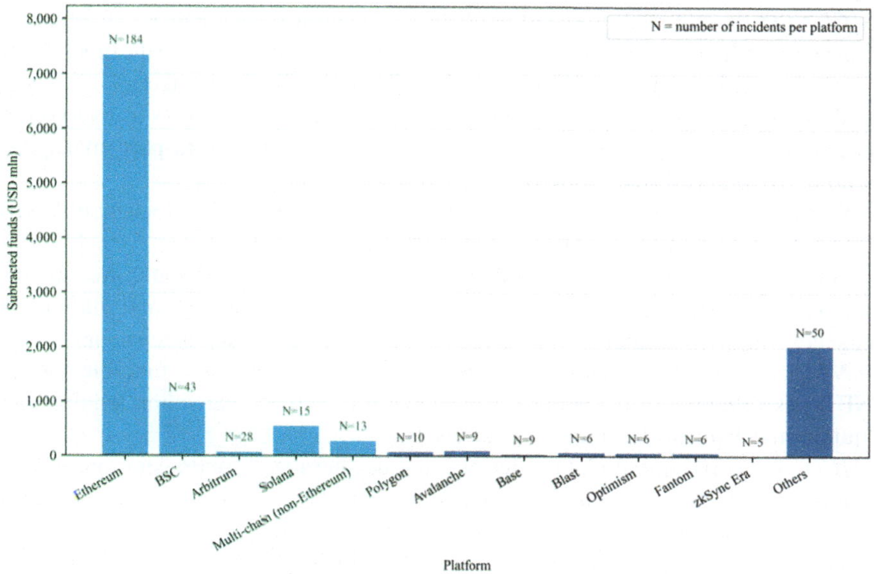

Fig. 4.3 Total losses per platforms

updated DeFi risk taxonomy in the remainder of the book, followed by a discussion of implications and possible policy and market responses (Table 4.5).

Accordingly, targets are classified into seven distinct categories:

DeFi Protocol (326 reports): set of smart contracts that provide financial services (lending, borrowing, trading, staking, yield farming, etc.) in a decentralized way, without intermediaries. Some examples are DEXs (decentralized exchanges), lending platforms, liquidity protocols.

Table 4.5 Number of incidents and total losses per target

Target type	Incidents (N)	Share of incidents (%)	Total loss (USD mln)	Share of total loss (%)	Average loss per incident (USD mln)
DeFi protocol	326	84.90	6668.788	57.00	20.456
CEX	33	8.59	4295.714	36.72	130.173
Other	14	3.65	513.577	4.39	36.684
Wallet	5	1.30	137.850	1.18	27.570
Gaming	3	0.78	70.700	0.60	23.567
ICO	1	0.26	7.700	0.07	7.700
NFTfi	1	0.26	5.000	0.04	5.000
DAO	1	0.26	0.120	0.00	0.120
Total	384	100.00	11,699.449	100.00	30.467

CEX (33 reports): "Centralized Exchange", a centralized exchange platform that manages user funds through direct custody. Transactions occur outside the blockchain and are managed by a controlling entity (e.g. Binance, Coinbase, etc.).

Wallet (5 reports): A service that manages private keys and allows users to send, receive, and store cryptocurrencies or NFTs. It can be custodial (third-party managed) or non-custodial (user-controlled).

Gaming (3 reports): Projects that integrate game mechanics with blockchain-based financial components (e.g. play-to-earn, in-game tokens, NFTs).

DAOs (1 signalling): "Decentralized Autonomous Organization", are organizational structures based on smart contracts that allow collective and automated management of on-chain resources through decentralized voting mechanism.

NFTfi (1 signalling): The set of DeFi protocols that use non-fungible tokens (NFTs) as collateral or the subject of financial transactions, extending lending and liquidity mechanisms to unique digital assets.

ICO (1 report): Initial Coin Offerings, are decentralized fundraising operations that involve the issuance of new digital tokens against cryptocurrencies, constituting a form of disintermediated financing native to blockchain (Fig. 4.4).

The target classification provides technical insights into where risk materialises within the observed incident sample. The predominance of cases involving DeFi protocols suggests that, in the available evidence, vulnerabilities are most frequently realised at the application layer, namely through smart-contract logic and the economic design of protocol mechanisms (e.g., AMMs, collateralisation and liquidation rules, oracle dependencies, incentive structures, and composability).

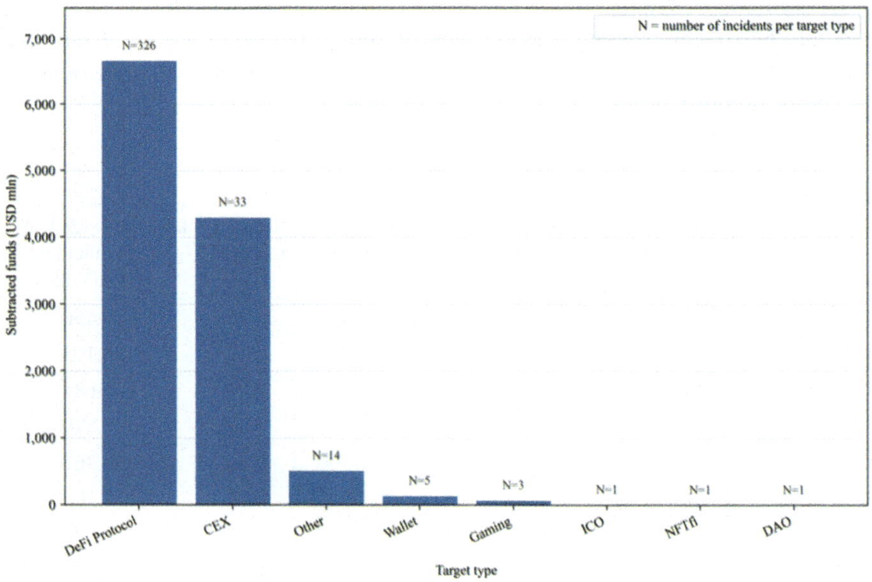

Fig. 4.4 Total losses per target

Conversely, the smaller number of CEX-related reports should not be interpreted as proportionately lower risk, but rather as a different risk profile in which losses tend to originate from custodial arrangements, operational controls, and governance failures, often characterised by concentration and single-point-of-failure dynamics. The remaining target categories (wallets, gaming, DAOs, NFTfi and ICOs) form a statistical long tail; given the limited number of observations, they do not support robust inference and may partly reflect reporting and measurement biases, since protocol exploits are typically more visible and systematically documented than other forms of misconduct. Overall, these patterns support focusing the quantitative indicator framework primarily on protocol-level exposures and vulnerabilities, while treating the residual target classes as contextual determinants of risk rather than as standalone quantitative clusters.

4.4 Attack Techniques

Table 4.6 shows the attack techniques statistics. The analysis reveals that, in the DeFi space, attackers use various attack techniques, some of which are more commonly employed than others. However, less frequent techniques sometimes allow attackers to steal larger amounts compared to more established methods.

In particular, the most common types of attacks are:

Private Key Compromised: 44 cases and $2985 million stolen. This attack method involves compromising a private key, where the cause is not clearly identifiable, but with evident effects such as unauthorized access, signing of malicious transactions, or altering the protocol's state, suggesting a potential supply chain vulnerability, human error, or undisclosed vector (Zhou et al., 2023).

Flashloan Price Oracle Attack: 28 cases and $424 million stolen. This technique involves manipulating price oracles (systems that provide quotes) through operations in AMM pools, exploited to deceive a protocol (e.g., lending) and acquire assets inappropriately (Cao et al., 2021).

Access Control Exploit: 18 cases and $752 million stolen. These are techniques in which an attacker exploits incorrect or missing access control mechanisms in a DeFi smart contract, gaining unauthorized privileges, altering the contract's state, or executing reserved functions, often due to missing Ownable modules, onlyOwner, require(), or poorly managed roles (Zhou et al., 2023).

Reentrancy: 19 cases and $154milion stolen. This is a vulnerability present in smart contracts that allows a function to be recursively called before the contract has updated its state, potentially allowing the misuse or repeated use of resources (Qian et al., 2025).

Combined Variants like Flashloan Reentrancy Attack: 17 cases and $179 milion stolen. These attacks combine flash loans, a type of instant or uncollateralized loan. A vulnerability in the smart contract is exploited to repeatedly call a function before its state is correctly updated (Cao et al., 2021).

Table 4.6 Number of incidents and total losses per attack methods

Attack technique	Incidents (N)	Share of incidents (%)	Total loss (USD mln)	Share of total loss (%)	Average loss per incident (USD mln)
Private key compromised	44	11.46	2985.441	25.52	67.851
Access control exploit	18	4.69	752.489	6.43	41.805
Flashloan price oracle attack	28	7.29	424.070	3.62	15.145
Flashloan reentrancy attack	17	4.43	179.090	1.53	10.535
Price oracle attack	10	2.60	176.479	1.51	17.648
Reentrancy	19	4.95	154.250	1.32	8.118
Drained contracts	13	3.39	152.320	1.30	11.717
Infinite mint and dump	7	1.82	68.800	0.59	9.829
Others	228	59.38	6806.510	58.18	29.853
Total	384	100.00	11,699.449	100.00	30.467

Drained Contracts: 13 cases and $152 milion stolen. This technique exploits logical vulnerabilities or unreversed privileges to drain funds from smart contracts, thus compromising the economic security of the protocol (Qian et al., 2025) (Fig. 4.5).

These categories reflect how hackers often combine technical vulnerabilities (software bugs) with financial manoeuvres (flash loans, market manipulation) to maximize profit. For example, in numerous observed attacks, the attacker borrowed large sums via flash loan, inflated the price of an asset he had bet on (pump) by manipulating an oracle, exploited the price divergence on another protocol to profit (dump), and repaid the loan all in a single sequence, leaving the target protocol with losses. Such flash attacks are difficult to prevent because they occur entirely on chain in seconds, leveraging the trustless composability of DeFi protocols. In addition to the most common techniques, the dataset shows that some rare methods produce very high average losses (Table 4.7).

For instance, several attack types appear only one or two times in the dataset but are associated with exceptionally large losses (> USD 100 million), including Safe Multisig wallet Phishing Exploit, Signature Exploit, Flashloan Governance Attack, Proof Verifier Bug, Spoof Token Exploit, Trusted Root Exploit, and Transfer Logic Exploit. In general, higher average profits per attack are associated with rarely used techniques, a sign that the most severe cases are often unique and not easily repeatable. This suggests a highly unbalanced distribution of hacker returns: most "routine"

Table 4.7 Number of incidents with N ≤ 2 and total loss > 100 USD mln per attack techniques

Attack technique	Incidents (N)	Share of incidents (%)	Total loss (USD mln)	Share of total loss (%)	Average loss per incident (USD mln)
Safe multisig wallet phishing exploit	2	0.52	1634.900	13.97	817.450
Proof verifier bug	1	0.26	570.000	4.87	570.000
Signature exploit	2	0.52	407.700	3.48	203.850
Spoof token exploit	1	0.26	223.000	1.91	223.000
Database attack	1	0.26	200.000	1.71	200.000
Trusted root exploit	1	0.26	190.000	1.62	190.000
Flashloan governance attack	1	0.26	181.000	1.55	181.000
Private key compromised (brute force)	2	0.52	160.865	1.37	80.433
Contract not initialized	1	0.26	150.000	1.28	150.000
Transfer logic exploit	2	0.52	101.000	0.86	50.500

exploits yield a few million, while a few exceptional events generate huge loot. A simple Pareto analysis confirms that 5% of the most serious incidents are responsible for approximately 60% of total recorded losses. Therefore, risk management must consider this "long tail" of catastrophic events, which pose special challenges (e.g. for the insurability of such risks).

4.5 Vulnerability and Fraud Classification

The classification of incidents according to the nature of vulnerability or abuse shows that only a limited number of categories are exploited. The descriptive statistics are reported in Table 4.8.

Protocol Logic is the most frequent class, with 184 cases (47.92%), and accounts for USD 5,087.850 million in losses (43.49% of total), with an average loss of USD

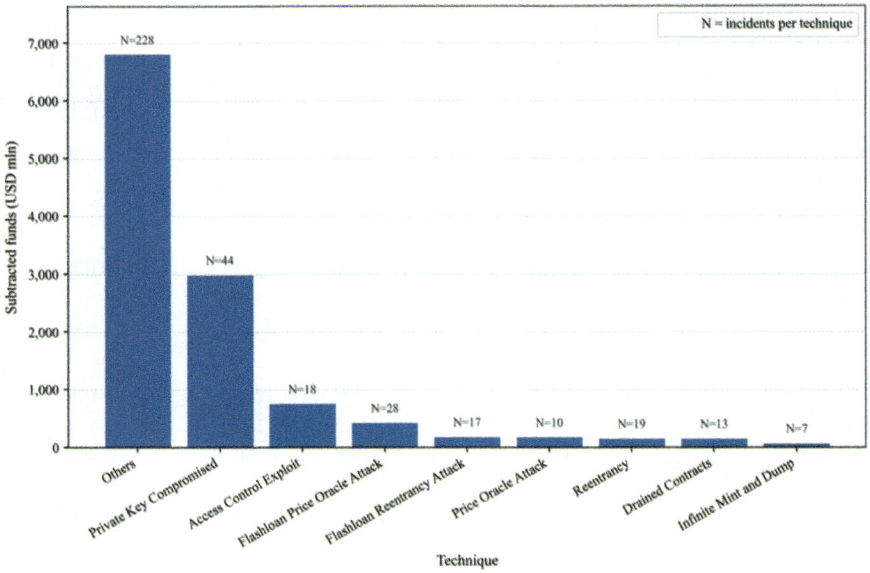

Fig. 4.5 Total losses per attack technique

Table 4.8 Number of incidents and total losses per type of frauds

Type of fraud	Incidents (N)	Share of incidents (%)	Total loss (USD mln)	Share of total loss (%)	Average loss per incident (USD mln)
Protocol logic	184	47.92	5087.850	43.49	27.651
Infrastructure	89	23.18	4958.181	42.38	55.710
Ecosystem	73	19.01	1189.627	10.17	16.296
Rugpull	27	7.03	253.146	2.16	9.376
Smart contract language	7	1.82	123.610	1.06	17.659
Others	4	1.04	87.035	0.74	21.759
Total	384	100.00	11,699.449	100.00	30.467

27.651 million per incident. This category captures exploits rooted in the operational design of DeFi mechanisms, where attackers leverage weaknesses in the way protocols translate financial rules into on-chain constraints (e.g., collateral and liquidation logic, accounting rules, incentive design, and composability), often without necessarily violating the formal syntax of the code (Wen, 2024). Infrastructure incidents are fewer in number, 89 cases (23.18%), yet their loss impact is comparable to Protocol Logic, totalling USD 4958.181 million (42.38% of total). The implied severity is markedly higher, with an average loss of USD 55.710 million per incident. This pattern is consistent with the role of bridges and other interoperability components as high-value targets: a limited number of failures can produce disproportionate losses because value is concentrated in a small set of contracts and operational processes. Representative episodes include large bridge exploits such as Ronin and Poly Network, which illustrate how validator compromise, key-management failures, and cross-chain message verification weaknesses can dominate outcomes even when the underlying protocol logic appears sound (FSB, 2024; Rettig et al., 2025). Ecosystem failures account for 73 cases (19.01%) but represent a smaller share of total losses—USD 1189.627 million (10.17%)—with an average loss of USD 16.296 million per incident. These events are better interpreted as system-level dislocations in which losses arise from broader breakdowns or shock episodes that propagate across protocols and markets, rather than from a single isolated exploit. In operational terms, they often reflect stress that emerges through interconnections across protocols, price oracles, liquidity pools, or cross-chain interactions, and may generate cascading effects across multiple layers of the DeFi architecture (Bekemeier, 2021). Finally, Rugpull incidents amount to 27 cases (7.03%) and USD 253.146 million in losses (2.16%), corresponding to an average loss of USD 9.376 million per incident. These cases are associated with insider misconduct, where developers or privileged actors exploit control over liquidity, token issuance, or administrative permissions to appropriate user funds and leave investors with impaired or worthless tokens (Nguyen et al., 2023). Although smaller in aggregate losses than technical exploit categories within this sample, rug pulls remain material from a conduct-risk perspective and are particularly relevant during phases of market exuberance. Industry evidence indicates that rug pulls surged during the 2021 cycle and represented a substantial share of scam activity in that period.

Two residual categories account for a small share of observations. Smart Contract Language incidents comprise 7 cases (1.82%) with $123.610 million in losses (1.06%) and an average loss of $17.659 million per incident. This class captures programming-level vulnerabilities and semantic or implementation errors in smart contract code (Zhou et al., 2023). Others include 4 cases (1.04%) totalling $87.035 million (0.74%) with an average loss of $21.759 million. Taken together, the distribution suggests that while protocol-logic exploits dominate by frequency, infrastructure failures drive a disproportionately large share of aggregate losses, reinforcing the need to treat bridge and interoperability components as systemically relevant attack surfaces alongside core protocol design (Fig. 4.6).

Overall, data show that, within DeFi, attackers employ numerous attack techniques, some of which are used more frequently than others. However, less common methods sometimes allow attackers to steal larger amounts compared to more established techniques. This has implications both for investors, who should be able to recognize signs of recurring scam activity, and for regulators, who are called upon to prioritize interventions in areas of greatest systemic risk (critical infrastructure and interconnections) without neglecting widespread user protection against widespread fraud.

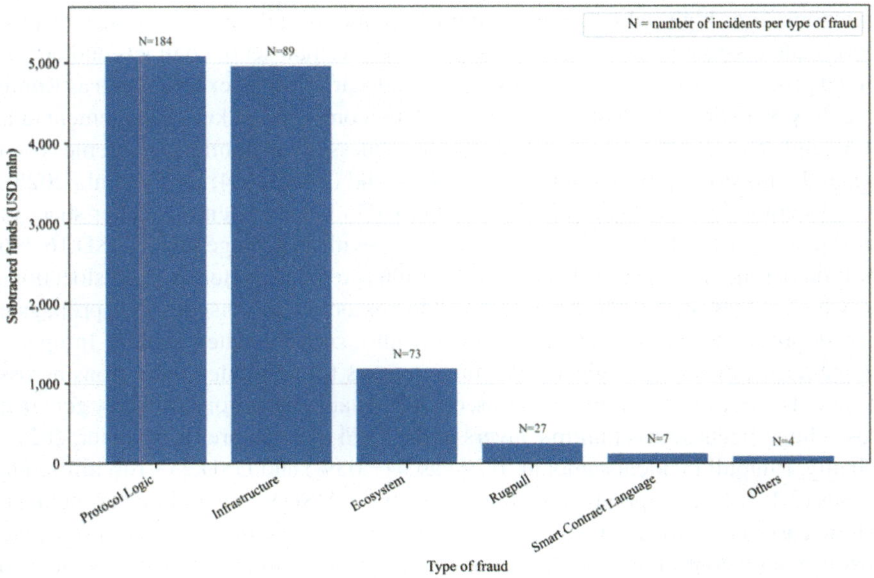

Fig. 4.6 Total losses per fraud type

4.6 Limitations

Several limitations should be acknowledged in interpreting the findings presented in this chapter. First, the analysis may be affected by survivorship bias. Protocols that have ceased operations following major incidents or have disappeared without formal reporting may be underrepresented in available datasets. As a result, the observable sample may disproportionately reflect projects that survived attacks or maintained sufficient visibility to be documented, potentially underestimating the full extent of structural fragilities within the ecosystem. Second, underreporting of minor incidents represents a constraint. Smaller exploits, partial fund drains, or governance abuses are not always publicly disclosed, particularly where project teams seek to avoid reputational damage or user panic. In decentralised environments lacking mandatory disclosure standards, transparency depends largely on voluntary reporting, third-party investigations, or community monitoring. Consequently, the empirical database may understate the frequency of low-value or "silent" events, leading to a possible downward bias in incident counts. Third, the use of Total Value Locked (TVL) as an analytical benchmark entails methodological caveats. TVL is typically calculated on a mark-to-market basis and is therefore sensitive to token price fluctuations, which may inflate or deflate perceived scale independently of underlying economic activity. Moreover, TVL captures on-chain locked assets but does not fully account for off-chain exposures, rehypothecation practices, or implicit leverage embedded in derivative or cross-protocol structures. As such, while TVL provides a useful aggregate indicator of ecosystem size and concentration, it should not be interpreted as a comprehensive measure of systemic exposure. These limitations call for cautious interpretation and highlight the need for improved data standardisation, disclosure practices, and integrated on- and off-chain monitoring tools in future research.

References

Bekemeier, F. (2021). Deceptive assurance? A conceptual view on systemic risk in decentralized finance (DeFi). In *ICBTA'21: Proceedings of the 2021 4th international conference on blockchain technology and applications* (pp. 76–87). https://doi.org/10.1145/3510487.3510499

Cao, Y., Zou, C., & Cheng, X. (2021). *Flashot: A snapshot of flash loan attack on DeFi ecosystem.* https://arxiv.org/abs/2102.00626

International Monetary Fund-Financial Stability Board (IMF-FSB). (2024). *G20 cryptoasset policy implementation roadmap, status report.* https://www.fsb.org/2024/10/g20-crypto-asset-policy-implementation-roadmap-status-report/

International Organization of Securities Commissions (IOSCO). (2023). *Policy recommendations for decentralized finance (DeFi).*

Nguyen, M. H., Huynh, P. D., Dau, S. H., & Li, X. (2023). Rug-pull malicious token detection on blockchain using supervised learning with feature engineering. In *Proceedings of the 2023 Australasian computer science week (ACSW '23)* (pp. 72–81).

Qian, P., Cao, R., Liu, Z., Li, W., Li, M., Zhang, L., Xu, Y., Chen, J., & He, Q. (2025). Comprehensive review of smart contract and DeFi security: Attack, vulnerability detection, and automated repair. *Expert Systems with Applications, 291*, 128431. https://doi.org/10.1016/j.eswa.2025.128431

Rettig, R., Mosier, M., & Gilman, K. (2025). Genuine DeFi as critical infrastructure: A conceptual framework for combating illicit finance activity in decentralized finance. *Journal of Financial Regulation, 11*(2), 215–253.

Wen, H., Liu, H., Song, J., Chen, Y., Guo, W., & Feng, Y. (2024). FORAY: Towards effective attack synthesis against deep logical vulnerabilities in DeFi protocols. In *Proceedings of the 2024 ACM SIGSAC Conference on Computer and Communications Security* (CCS '24) (pp. 1–15). ACM.

Zhou, L., Xiong, X., Ernstberger, J., Chaliasos, S., Wang, Z., Wang, Y., Qin, K., Wattenhofer, R., Song, D., & Gervais, A. (2023). *SoK: Decentralized finance (DeFi) attacks.* https://arxiv.org/abs/2208.13035

Chapter 5
A Proposal for a New DeFi Risks Taxonomy

Abstract Empirical observation necessitates conceptual refinement. Drawing upon both the theoretical architecture and the incident data, this chapter advances a revised taxonomy of DeFi-related risks. While retaining alignment with established financial risk classifications, it introduces additional categories designed to capture vulnerabilities intrinsic to protocol-based systems. The objective is analytical precision: to map observable failure modes onto their structural determinants in code, governance, and infrastructure. The chapter further proposes illustrative indicators that may assist supervisory authorities and policymakers in developing more coherent and comparable assessments of decentralized risk exposures.

* * *

Building on the risk taxonomy set out in IOSCO (2023) and discussed in Chapter 1, this section proposes a more granular classification of DeFi incidents that moves beyond a narrow focus on financial risk categories. Alongside market and liquidity risks, the analysis incorporates technical vulnerabilities, governance failures, misconduct dynamics, and structural weaknesses inherent in protocol design. The aim is to develop a multidimensional framework capable of capturing not only the financial impact of DeFi incidents but also the operational, behavioural, and systemic conditions that shape their emergence and transmission. More specifically, the proposed classification integrates traditional financial risk concepts with the technological and infrastructural features characteristic of protocol-based intermediation. It adopts a multilevel approach. Where analytically appropriate, DeFi risks are mapped onto established financial risk categories, consistent with the principle of "same activity, same risk, same regulation." At the same time, distinct categories are introduced to reflect risks that arise uniquely from decentralised architectures, such as smart contract dependencies oracle fragility, and governance manipulation. The section also illustrates how this risk categories can be operationalised through indicative quantitative metrics, enabling a more systematic assessment of frequency, severity, and structural relevance.

L. Barbaro et al., *Crypto and Decentralized Finance Under Stress*,
SpringerBriefs in Finance, https://doi.org/10.1007/978-3-032-28425-9_5

5.1 Financial Market and Liquidity Risks

This category includes cryptocurrency price volatility, risk of market collapses (rapid drawdowns), and liquidity problems in decentralized markets (thin order books, liquidity-concentrating AMM pools). These risks mirror traditional market risks but can be amplified by the lack of stabilization mechanisms (e.g., market makers of last resort) and the 24/7 non-stop nature of crypto markets. DeFi also includes run risks on key assets (e.g., redemption runs on algorithmic stablecoins) and the possibility of market manipulation through coordinated on-chain actions (orchestrated DEX pumps and dumps, oracle manipulation attacks that cause temporary price distortions, etc.). More in detail, on one hand, price volatility in cryptoassets is not merely higher in magnitude; it is also more persistent and more rapidly transmitted across interconnected markets through automated liquidation mechanisms and collateral dependencies. On the other hand, liquidity risk is structurally embedded in AMM models, where liquidity is endogenous and concentrated in specific pools rather than distributed across layered order books.

Some quantitative indicators can be employed to estimate and monitor these market and liquidity risks in a systematic manner. In particular, volatility-based and liquidity-sensitive measures allow for an assessment of both pure price risk and the additional losses that may arise under stressed trading conditions. The following indicators represent illustrative tools that can be used within a DeFi-specific risk-monitoring framework:

- *Value at Risk* (VaR). VaR is a quantile-based risk measure that estimates the loss threshold that will not be exceeded over a given time horizon with a specified confidence level (e.g., 99%), under the assumptions of the chosen model. VaR can be computed using different approaches, including parametric (often relying on distributional assumptions such as normality), historical simulation (non-parametric), or Monte Carlo simulation. It is widely used to summarise market (price) risk, but standard VaR typically does **not** incorporate liquidity effects such as slippage and market impact. In the DeFi context, VaR can help assess the sensitivity of lending protocols, liquidity providers, and leveraged positions whose solvency depends on collateral values. For example, an increase in the VaR of a major collateral asset can act as an early-warning indicator of rising liquidation risk across lending platforms. Because DeFi protocols rely on predefined collateralisation ratios, higher short-term volatility mechanically increases the likelihood of margin calls and forced liquidations. VaR can therefore be applied not only at the portfolio level but also at the protocol level to approximate stress thresholds under adverse market conditions. However, VaR alone may be insufficient in decentralised markets, where liquidity can deteriorate abruptly and amplify realised losses, particularly in AMM-based environments, where slippage depends on pool depth and trade size and where liquidity may be concentrated or withdrawn rapidly in response to changing incentives (Heimbach & Huang, 2024).

- *Liquidity-Adjusted Value at Risk* (L-VaR). This measure extends VaR to include liquidity risk. It combines the volatility of returns with that of the bid-ask spread. This indicator is especially pertinent in DeFi settings. By incorporating bid-ask spread dynamics or price impact functions into the risk estimate, L-VaR captures the additional loss that arises when positions must be sold off under stressed liquidity conditions. L-VaR in DeFi can be measured with on-chain metrics such as pool depth, concentration ratios within liquidity pools, historical slippage under large trades, and volatility of liquidity provision. For lending protocols, L-VaR can help quantify the combined effect of collateral price declines and declining market depth during liquidation shocks. For decentralised exchanges, it can signal vulnerability to sudden liquidity withdrawals or to coordinated market manipulation strategies. Because DeFi markets operate continuously without circuit breakers, liquidity stress can emerge and propagate rapidly, making liquidity-adjusted measures more informative than traditional volatility-based metrics alone.
- *Cost of Liquidity* (CoL). The CoL is the exogenous cost of liquidity, calculated as half of the relative bid-ask spread, multiplied by the liquidated position. It reflects how much it costs to exit a position under stressed market conditions. It is a direct indicator of liquidity risk. CoL peaks often correspond to trend reversals in the market, suggesting that it can be used as an early warning indicator for financial instability. CoL acquires particular analytical relevance in decentralised finance, where liquidity provision is structurally endogenous and highly sensitive to market incentives. In DeFi, liquidity of AMM pools depends on the capital committed by liquidity providers, who can withdraw funds rapidly in response to several market conditions. Under specific circumstances, bid–ask spreads may suddenly widen and consequent slippage may increase non-linearly with trade size (Cartea et al., 2025). Measuring the CoL therefore provides a direct assessment of the cost of selling positions when liquidity deteriorates. Monitoring the evolution of CoL can allow supervisors or protocol designers to detect phases of tightening liquidity, particularly when increases in CoL are not solely attributable to higher volatility but to shrinking pool depth or liquidity concentration.

5.2 Credit and Leverage Risks

This category captures the risk of default and forced liquidation on DeFi lending platforms, as well as the amplification effects associated with intensive leverage (including recursive borrowing and compounding strategies). In decentralised lending, credit risk is largely mechanised: collateral constraints and liquidation rules are executed by smart contracts and external liquidators. As a result, abrupt price moves can trigger synchronised liquidations, potentially reinforcing market stress through feedback effects and execution frictions. Empirical evidence shows that liquidation activity can become highly clustered in time and across collateral types, with protocol outcomes depending not only on price dynamics but also on execution conditions and market depth (Qin et al., 2021a, 2021b; Lehar, 2022; Heimbach & Huang, 2024).

Non-traditional collateral (e.g., LP tokens and synthetic assets) can further increase fragility, since its value may deteriorate sharply precisely when liquidation demand peaks. Finally, adversarial strategies—most notably oracle and price-manipulation attacks, often facilitated by flash loans—can induce artificial undercollateralisation and liquidations even in the absence of fundamental shocks (Mackinga et al., 2022).

A compact set of indicators is sufficient to monitor this risk category in a way that is both operational and comparable across protocols:

- *Liquidation proximity* (system-wide margin tightness). The distribution of positions' distance to the liquidation threshold (e.g., share of accounts with a small buffer above the trigger) provides an ex-ante measure of how much of the system can be liquidated by a modest adverse move (Qin et al., 2021a, 2021b; Lehar, 2022).
- *Liquidation pressure and concentration.* Liquidation volume relative to outstanding borrows, together with concentration across collateral assets and time (stress-window clustering), captures the likelihood of liquidation cascades and the scope for market-impact amplification (Qin et al., 2021a, 2021b; Lehar, 2022).
- *Bad-debt ratio* (losses after liquidation). Bad debt as a share of total borrows is the cleanest realised measure of credit losses at protocol level. It isolates cases in which liquidation proceeds fail to cover outstanding debt, which is typically associated with liquidity shortfalls and delayed execution under stress (Qin et al., 2021a, 2021b; Chiu et al., 2023).

Leverage build-up. Leverage proxies based on collateralised borrowing activity, capturing recursive/compounding strategies, summarise the system's sensitivity to volatility and funding conditions and help identify phases of risk accumulation prior to stress events (Heimbach & Huang, 2024).

5.3 Operational and Technological Risks

These collect all technical vulnerabilities of protocols and decentralized infrastructure. They are ideally divided into two subclasses:

(i) protocol code and logic vulnerabilities—bugs in smart contracts, logical errors in financial formulas or access controls (protocol logic), incorrect implementations that can be exploited (such as reentrancy, integer overflow/underflow, bypassable signature checks);
(ii) infrastructure and cybersecurity vulnerabilities—compromise of private keys (admin wallets or multi-sigs), attacks on cross-chain bridges (which often rely on validators or federated custodians), exploits on external services on which

the protocol depends (oracle providers, APIs), and attacks on developers' or users' hardware/software platforms (supply chain attacks, malware, etc.).

This macro-category is peculiar to DeFi and ultimately represents the IT/cyber risks of a financial system devoid of human intermediaries, where "code is law". The data shows that this includes both frequent but minor events (bug exploits on small protocols) and rare but devastating events (e.g. infrastructure hacks such as bridges with hundreds of millions of damages). Some quantitative indicators useful for measuring this type of risk are:

- *Average time to first hack* (Time-To-Exploit). The time between the launch of a protocol and its first security incident. A short "average compromise time" would indicate that many protocols are hacked shortly after launch (perhaps due to rushed development at the expense of security).[1] This parameter helps assess the initial resilience of the code: for example, protocols with very low Time-To-Exploit may indicate poor development practices or insufficient audits.
- *Frequency and severity of technical exploits.* Number of attacks/hacks per unit of time (e.g. quarterly) and average amount of losses. For example: the number of attacks occurring each quarter and the mean and maximum funds subtracted to detect temporal trends in technical vulnerability. This sort of indicators can support in monitoring whether bugs in smart contract codes are increasing or decreasing and help to assess the financial impact. An increase in the number of exploits or average losses over time suggests greater technical risk in DeFi.
- *Vulnerability index by attack type.* A structured assessment of protocol fragility can be obtained by examining the distribution of incidents across technical attack categories such as re-entrancy exploits, flash loan attacks, oracle manipulation, bridge exploits, and similar vectors, and by measuring their corresponding share of total financial losses. The joint analysis of frequency and loss magnitude provides a more informative proxy of systemic vulnerability than simple incident counts. Drawing on the empirical evidence presented in Chapter 4, the relative incidence of specific attack methods, combined with the aggregate funds extracted through each method, allows for an estimation of their structural relevance. For instance, if 7.5% of documented exploits involve flash loan–based oracle manipulation but account for only 2.7% of total losses, this suggests that such attacks are relatively frequent but tend to generate limited financial damage on average. Conversely, other attack vectors such as large-scale bridge exploits or complex flash loan arbitrage attacks, may occur less frequently yet result in disproportionately high losses. Then, an analytically useful metric in this context is the average loss per attack type, which captures the expected financial impact conditional on the occurrence of a specific exploit category. This indicator can help to identify which technical vulnerabilities are not merely recurrent but also economically destructive. When combined with frequency measures, it enables the construction of a composite vulnerability index capable of distinguishing between high-frequency/

---

[1] TRM Labs: "*Category deep-dive: $2.2 billion was stolen in crypto-related hacks in 2024*". Avaiable at: https://www.trmlabs.com.

low-severity risks and low-frequency/high-severity systemic threats (Li et al., 2022; Weingärtner, 2023).

5.4 Risks of Fraud and Unlawful Conduct

This risk category encompasses all cases in which human actors exploit the DeFi ecosystem for fraudulent or abusive purposes. It includes rug pulls and Ponzi schemes orchestrated by rogue developers; front-running practices and malicious forms of Miner/Maximal Extractable Value (MEV), such as sandwich attacks in which bots intercept and reorder transactions to extract value at users' expense; wash trading and market manipulation on unsupervised decentralised exchanges (DEXs); and the laundering of illicit proceeds through mixers, DEXs, and pseudonymous DeFi platforms. This category partially overlaps with operational risk. However, certain structural features of DeFi (i.e., the absence of KYC requirements, pseudonymity, and the lack of centralised surveillance mechanisms) may facilitate the proliferation of such misconduct. The impact of these behaviours is twofold. First, they generate direct financial losses for affected users, as illustrated by cases such as the approximately USD 60 million stolen from AnubisDAO (Zhang et al., 2023) and the substantial amounts lost in fraudulent yield farming schemes. Second, they create reputational and market integrity risks that may undermine confidence in decentralised markets and trigger significant regulatory intervention if left unaddressed. Some relevant indicators associated with this risk category include:

- *Anonymity vs. Risk Index.* A qualitative-quantitative parameter that correlates the anonymity of a project team with the likelihood of misconduct. One could encode each protocol with a score of "team transparency" (e.g. 0 = anonymous team, 1 = partially known team, 2 = public and verified team) and empirically verify the correlation with conduct incidents. The resulting indicator could be the frequency of rug pulls by team category: if most rug pulls are associated with anonymous teams, then the presence of a public team could be considered risk mitigation. This approach is supported by the observation that team accountability and the risks associated with anonymity are key factors: the variable "Is the team public or anonymous?" is in fact considered in DeFi risk assessment frameworks. A high number of frauds from unidentifiable developers underscores the importance of including this indicator in risk models.
- *Concentration of wealth and dumping risk*: Distribution of tokens and economic power within a protocol, to identify potential abuses. A quantitative indicator is the Gini coefficient or Herfindahl index applied to the distribution of governance/liquidity tokens among holders. For example, if the top 1% of addresses hold > 90% of a token, there is a high risk of dumping or market manipulation by a few actors (which falls under the risks of opportunistic conduct). For each project, the percentage of supply held by the first 10 addresses can be calculated and an alert threshold defined (e.g. "Concentration index > 0.5" or " > 80% token in 10 addresses" indicates high conduct risk). This reflects vulnerability to exit scam:

if founders or a few whales[2] hold nearly all the value, they can liquidate their positions, causing price crashes and losses for smaller users.

- *Confidence Index versus Abnormal Return* (Red Flag Yield). An empirical parameter that relates the promised returns of a protocol to measures of confidence and sustainability. Fraudulent schemes often offer an unusually high Annual Percentage Yield (APY); an indicator can then be created that signals protocols with APYs that are out of scale with the market average and combined with other factors (no audits, anonymous team, low TVL, and high concentration) to highlight potential fraudulent projects. For example, if a small protocol offers > 1000% APY without a clear revenue model, the indicator would have a high value. This is a quantitative/preventive approach: a cluster of protocols with abnormal returns and poor transparency metrics can be identified through data clustering and flagged as high conduct risk.
- *Reported versus Real Incident Rate* (Dark Figure Index). This indicator seeks to approximate the extent to which fraudulent or abusive events remain unreported in official or widely cited databases. By comparing observable on-chain anomalies with incidents formally documented by sources such as Rekt or DeFiLlama, it is possible to estimate a "dark figure" of unrecorded events. A significant gap between detected on-chain irregularities and publicly reported incidents would suggest systematic underreporting. This may be particularly relevant for smaller protocols, where minor rug pulls, silent exit scams, or low-value exploitations may not attract public disclosure or media attention. In such cases, the perceived level of misconduct risk could materially underestimate the actual scale of abusive behaviour within the ecosystem. By capturing discrepancies between observable blockchain data and documented incidents, the Dark Figure Index can help to provide a complementary perspective on conduct risk and enhances the robustness of early-warning assessments.

5.5 Governance and Centralization Risks

This category concerns vulnerabilities that stem from partial, nominal, or misleading forms of decentralisation. Many protocols present themselves as decentralised, yet decision-making power may remain concentrated in a limited number of actors. High concentration of governance tokens, privileged administrative keys, and opaque or weakly safeguarded voting procedures can introduce structural fragilities that are not immediately visible to users. Where governance tokens are heavily concentrated, control over protocol decisions can be effectively captured. An actor acquiring a sufficient share, whether through market purchases, coordinated accumulation, or temporary borrowing, may influence or determine voting outcomes and introduce

[2] The term whales refers to individuals or entities that hold an extremely large amount of a given digital asset, allowing them to significantly influence its liquidity and price performance on the market.

changes detrimental to users. Such governance attacks can result in several problems like parameter manipulation, treasury extraction, or modifications that weaken protocol safeguards.

A further vulnerability arises from upgradeable smart contracts controlled by administrative keys. If core developers or a small group retain unilateral authority to modify code, the system's trust assumptions shift from protocol logic to human discretion. Should those keys be compromised, the attacker may alter contract behaviour and redirect funds, circumventing the protections embedded in on-chain execution. The existence of these "backdoors" undermines the premise of trust minimisation that underpins decentralised architectures. Monitoring can focus on measurable proxies of decentralisation. Relevant indicators may include:

- *Governance Decentralization Index*: A quantitative measure of how distributed a protocol's decision-making process is. A proxy is the administrative control index: it evaluates the extent to which protocol changes depend on restricted admin keys or multi-sigs[3] rather than decentralized processes. For each protocol, a score can be defined: 0 = controlled by a single administrator (single private key), 0.5 = controlled by multi-sigs (M-of-N signatures[4]), 1 = fully decentralized control via on-chain voting without privileged keys. A low value (close to zero) signals high structural centralization: the protocol can be modified or closed by a few individuals, with a risk of abuse or human error. For example, if only 19% of the DeFi protocols analysed use multi-sig to protect administration keys[5] this means that over'80% still rely on centralized controls (often single hot wallet keys), a major vulnerability. This metric can also be presented as an aggregate "Key Security Index" for the industry.
- *Oracle Concentration Index and Infrastructure*: Many protocols depend on common services such as price oracles (e.g. Chainlink) or cloud infrastructure/ APIs. A quantitative indicator is the share of protocols using the same primary oracle. If, for example, 8 out of 10 protocols use Chainlink for pricing, then a malfunction or attack on Chainlink would have a systemic impact. An Oracle Concentration Index (similar to the previous HHI but for oracle providers) can be defined: high values = structural vulnerability. Similarly, a Cloud Dependency Score could estimate how many protocols use centralized providers (Infura, Alchemy, AWS services) for critical operations. These indicators reveal off-blockchain but crucial dependencies: recent incidents show that attacks on

[3] Multi-sig (multi-signature) is a cryptographic security mechanism that requires the digital signature of multiple private keys to authorize a transaction or change the state of a smart contract. Unlike traditional single-key management, this system distributes control across multiple parties, reducing the risk of funds being compromised or misused.

[4] The M-of-N signature model is an authorization mechanism used in multi-signature (multi-sig) systems, where an operation is valid only if at least M digital signatures are provided on a total of N possible signatories. This scheme allows control to be distributed across multiple parties, reducing the risk of unauthorized access or abuse of power by a single actor. For example, in a 3-of-5 configuration, three out of five signatories must approve the transaction for it to be executed.

[5] Breaking Down the Top 100 DeFi Hacks: https://www.halborn.com/reports/top-100-defi-hacks-2025.

API keys or internet infrastructure can compromise DeFi protocols without affecting smart contracts (e.g., exploits via compromised API keys). Monitoring concentration on a few suppliers helps identify latent operational risks.

5.6 Interconnection, Contagion and Systemic Risks

This category captures the possibility that localised shocks within DeFi may propagate through the system via cascading and contagion mechanisms. While systemic risk and financial contagion are well-established concepts in traditional finance, the structural features of DeFi, its modular design, composability, high degree of asset interdependence, and global accessibility, create distinct transmission channels. Protocols are frequently layered on top of one another, share collateral assets, and rely on common liquidity pools, so that stress in one component may rapidly affect others. A triggering event, such as the exploitation of a foundational protocol or the sharp devaluation of a key asset, including a widely used stablecoin, can initiate a sequence of reactions across multiple platforms. Liquidation cascades in lending protocols, redemption runs, temporary or persistent peg deviations, and cross-protocol insolvencies are typical manifestations of such dynamics. Because smart contracts execute automatically and markets operate continuously, these feedback loops can unfold at high speed and without discretionary intervention. Concentration further amplifies systemic exposure. A substantial share of DeFi collateral is often denominated in a limited set of assets, such as ETH, USDT, or wBTC. Heavy reliance on a small number of tokens increases the likelihood that distress affecting one asset will transmit across the broader ecosystem.

Furthermore, this risk category warrants distinct treatment within the taxonomy. Unlike operational or governance failures, systemic risk requires macroprudential monitoring tools capable of capturing network effects and aggregate vulnerabilities. Relevant instruments may include network-based stress testing, simulations of liquidation cascades, and indicators of aggregate leverage and collateral concentration.

The potential relevance of these dynamics extends beyond the boundaries of DeFi. International bodies have cautioned that, if sufficiently large and interconnected, decentralised markets could transmit shocks to traditional finance. Although, at present, DeFi and traditional financial systems remain largely separated, ongoing integration, including the entry of banks of other financial institutions into crypto-related activities and the tokenisation of real-world assets, may increase cross-sector linkages. In that scenario, the mitigation of systemic risk within DeFi would assume greater importance for the resilience of the whole financial system.

The following indicators provide illustrative metrics for assessing these risks:

- *Systemic Impact Score*. An interesting approach is to simulate contagion scenarios: for example, virtually causing "collapsing" an important protocol and calculating how many and which other protocols would experience liquidity losses or cascading insolvencies. From these simulations, an indicator such as the Systemic

Impact Score for each protocol can be derived, defined as the aggregate percentage loss in the system caused by the default of that protocol. A high value implies that the protocol is deeply interlocked with others (e.g. a hypothetical default of MakerDAO or Aave could cause liquidations on various platforms). These quantitative stress tests, performed with network analysis techniques and flow models, empirically quantify latent systemic risk and help identify critical nodes to monitor.
- *Bridge Concentration Index.* Similar to exposure to common assets, measure how much the system relies on a few major bridges. If, for example, 80% of cross-chain traffic passes through just 2 bridges, they become systemic single points of failure. The indicator can be the market share of the top N bridges in total cross-chain volume: high values = structural vulnerability (see section below) with systemic repercussions.
- *Coordinated Shock Exposure.* Percentage of assets/TVL in common between protocols. For example, if many protocols share the same stablecoin as the basis of their reserves, the Common Asset Exposure quantifies that concentration. One possible indicator is the percentage of TVL dependent on the top 3 common assets. For example, if a large portion of DeFi value is supported by a few assets (e.g. USDC, ETH), systemic risk increases because the collapse of one of them would simultaneously affect many protocols.

This revised taxonomy of DeFi risks offers an integrated framework that combines traditional financial risk categories, adapted to a decentralised environment, with the operational, technological, governance, and conduct-related vulnerabilities specific to protocol-based systems. Such a mapping exercise provides a proposal basis for the design of targeted mitigation strategies and for the identification of early-warning indicators capable of signalling emerging fragilities. Nevertheless, the proposed indicators are subject to important limitations. Many rely primarily on publicly observable on-chain data, which, despite its transparency, does not fully capture off-chain agreements, undisclosed governance arrangements, informal coordination among actors, or incidents that remain unreported. Metrics such as VaR, liquidity-adjusted measures, or concentration indices depend heavily on modelling assumptions and parameter calibration and may fail to capture extreme tail events in environments characterised by structural breaks and regime shifts. Network-based stress simulations, while informative, inevitably simplify the topology of inter-protocol dependencies and often abstract from behavioural feedback, endogenous liquidity withdrawals, or discretionary governance interventions. In addition, the rapid evolution of DeFi architectures implies that indicators calibrated on historical patterns may lose predictive power as new incentive schemes, cross-chain infrastructures, or attack vectors emerge.

These constraints suggest several directions for future research. First, greater effort should be devoted to integrating on-chain analytics with off-chain qualitative information, including governance documentation, audit quality, developer concentration, and legal structuring, in order to construct hybrid risk indicators. Second, the development of dynamic network models that incorporate behavioural responses, such as liquidity flight, governance voting shifts, or collateral reallocation, would improve the realism of systemic stress testing. Third, empirical work could examine the predictive validity of proposed early-warning metrics by testing their ability to anticipate large-scale incidents or market-wide stress episodes. Fourth, comparative analysis between DeFi and traditional financial contagion mechanisms may help refine the "same activity, same risk" principle in a macroprudential context.

References

Cartea, Á., Drissi, F., & Monga, M. (2025). Decentralised finance and automated market making: Execution and speculation. *Journal of Economic Dynamics and Control, 2025*, 105134.

Chiu, J., Ozdenoren, E., Yuan, K., & Zhang, S. (2023). *On the fragility of DeFi lending* (Staff Working Paper No. 2023–14). Bank of Canada.

Heimbach, L., & Huang, W. (2024). *DeFi leverage*. BIS working papers no. 117. Bank for International Settlements.

International Organization of Securities Commissions (IOSCO). (2023). *Policy recommendations for decentralized finance (DeFi).*

Lehar, A., & Parlour, C. A. (2022). *Systemic fragility in decentralised markets*. BIS working papers no. 1062. Bank for International Settlements.

Li, W., Bu, J., Li, X., & Chen, X. (2022). Security analysis of DeFi: Vulnerabilities, attacks and advances. *arXiv*. https://arxiv.org/abs/2205.09524.

Mackinga, T., Nadahalli, T., & Wattenhofer, R. (2022). TWAP oracle attacks: Easier done than said? *IACR cryptology ePrint archive*, 2022/445.

Qin, K., Lazzaretti, L., Zhou, L., Gervais, A., & Afonin, Y. (2021a). *CeFi vs. DeFi: Comparing centralized to decentralized finance*. https://arxiv.org/abs/2106.08157

Qin, K., Zhou, L., Gamito, P., Jovanovic, P., & Gervais, A. (2021b). An empirical study of DeFi liquidations: Incentives, risks, and instabilities. In *Proceedings of the ACM internet measurement conference (IMC'21)*. ACM.

Weingärtner, T., Fasser, F., Reis Sá da Costa, P., & Farkas, W. (2023). Deciphering DeFi: A Comprehensive Analysis and Visualization of Risks in Decentralized Finance. *Journal of Risk and Financial Management, 16*(10), 454. https://doi.org/10.3390/jrfm16100454

Zhang, Z., Lin, Z., Morales, M., Zhang, X., & Zhang, K. (2023). Your exploit is mine: Instantly synthesizing counterattack smart contract. In *Proceedings of the 32nd USENIX security symposium (USENIX Security 23).*

Chapter 6
Mixers as Risk Multipliers in the DeFi Ecosystem

Abstract Crypto mixers occupy a liminal position within the decentralized landscape, situated at the intersection of legitimate privacy interests and regulatory concern. In the aftermath of security breaches, they frequently serve as mechanisms for obfuscating transaction trails and redistributing misappropriated assets across chains. The 2022 Ronin Bridge exploit provides a paradigmatic case through which to examine these dynamics. By tracing the interaction between cross-chain infrastructures and mixing services, this chapter illuminates a structural tension: the same architectural features that enhance autonomy and censorship resistance may simultaneously complicate compliance and enforcement. Mixers thus emerge as a boundary infrastructure in both technical and normative terms.

* * *

6.1 Mixer Definition and Functioning

Within the broader DeFi risk landscape, mixers represent an additional and increasingly relevant source of vulnerability (Tippe & Deckers, 2025). While not constituting a standalone risk category, they affect the overall risk profile of the ecosystem by altering the conditions under which misconduct can be detected, traced, and sanctioned. Mixers are designed to enhance transactional privacy by pooling and redistributing cryptoassets in ways that sever the direct link between sender and recipient addresses. In doing so, they introduce an additional layer of opacity into an environment that is otherwise characterised by public ledger transparency. This functionality has important implications for risk dynamics. By weakening traceability, mixers complicate post-incident investigations and reduce the likelihood of asset recovery following hacks, fraud, or exploit events. Empirical evidence from the analysis of 384 DeFi attacks between 2016 and 2025 (see Chapter 4) shows that only nine incidents resulted in partial fund recovery (see Table 6.1). The low recovery rate is closely associated with the systematic use of mixing services to obscure illicit flows. Although originally motivated by privacy concerns, mixers have increasingly

L. Barbaro et al., *Crypto and Decentralized Finance Under Stress*,
SpringerBriefs in Finance, https://doi.org/10.1007/978-3-032-28425-9_6

Table 6.1 Funds recovered post-attack

Date	DeFi protocols	Subtracted amount	Recovered amount	%
19/04/2020	dForce	$ 25,000.000	$ 5000.000	20.00
03/09/2021	Siren	$ 3450.000	$ 850.000	24.64
29/10/2021	AnubisDAO	$ 60,000.000	$ 222.634	0.37
04/12/2021	Bitmart	$ 196,000.000	$ 6750.000	3.44
09/08/2022	Curve DEX	$ 575.000	$ 575.000	100.00
06/11/2022	Pando rings	$ 22,000.000	$ 2100.000	9.55
18/08/2023	Exactly	$ 7200.000	$ 465.000	6.46
25/08/2023	Magnate finance	$ 6400.000	$ 300.000	4.69
01/02/2025	Sirio finance	2000.000	1600.000	80.00

Fig. 6.1 Operation of mixers

become instrumental in laundering stolen assets and shielding malicious actors from identification.[1] In this sense, mixers do not create new risks, but materially amplify operational, conduct, and systemic risks by eroding the effectiveness of enforcement and deterrence mechanisms within the DeFi ecosystem.

As anticipated, mixers operate by receiving cryptoassets from multiple users, aggregating them into a common pool, and subsequently redistributing the funds to newly generated addresses, thereby significantly reducing the ability to link original inputs to final outputs (Fig. 6.1).

A prominent example is Tornado Cash, which relies on smart contracts combined with zero-knowledge proof cryptography[2] to enable withdrawals that cannot be directly linked to the original deposits. In operational terms, users deposit fixed-denomination into a specific pool and receive a cryptographic note. At a later stage, they can use this note to prove, through a zero-knowledge proof, that they are entitled to withdraw funds from the pool without revealing which specific deposit corresponds to their claim. The crucial feature is that the validity of the withdrawal is verified without disclosing the transaction-level link between input and output

[1] Elliptic analysis at: https://www.elliptic.co/resources/regulatory-outlook-2022.

[2] Zero-knowledge proofs are cryptographic protocols that allow one party (the prover) to prove to another party (the verifier) that they know or possess certain information-such as a secret key or the validity of a transaction-without revealing any details of the information itself. This mechanism is based on mathematical principles that allow the correctness of a statement to be verified in a probabilistically certain way, while preserving the confidentiality of the underlying data. In blockchain and DeFi, ZKPs are used to ensure privacy, scalability, and transaction integrity, as in the zk-SNARK and zk-STARK protocols, which allow off-chain validation of large amounts of data with minimal impact on the network's computational load.

addresses. While the underlying blockchain remains transparent, the cryptographic construction effectively breaks on-chain traceability between depositor and withdrawal addresses absent additional side-channel information. This mechanism, originally developed to enhance transactional privacy in public ledgers, significantly complicates forensic reconstruction once illicit funds have entered the mixing pool. As reported in Table 6.2, Ethereum accounts for the highest concentration of mixer deployments, although similar implementations are now present on BSC, Polygon, Arbitrum, and Solana.

Ethereum continues to represent the principal ecosystem in which mixing services have reached operational maturity and meaningful scale. This predominance is closely linked to its historical centrality within DeFi and to the substantial liquidity available on the network, both of which enhance its attractiveness for privacy-oriented transactions and, in certain cases, for laundering illicit proceeds. At the same time, the expansion of mixers across alternative blockchains highlights the increasingly cross-chain character of the phenomenon. Several services are classified as "active limited," a status that may reflect reduced liquidity, partial functionality, or intensified regulatory scrutiny. Others remain at an experimental stage, particularly in ecosystems with different technical architectures. Taken together, these developments indicate that mixers are not confined to a single network but tend to follow liquidity flows and user activity across platforms. From a supervisory standpoint, this dispersion complicates oversight and facilitates the rapid migration of illicit funds between chains, thereby weakening the effectiveness of enforcement measures confined to a specific jurisdiction or blockchain. Illicit use of mixers generally follows two distinct patterns (Fig. 6.2).

The first is source obfuscation, whereby illicit actors route stolen or otherwise illegal proceeds through a mixer before transferring the funds to a centralised exchange, often in combination with private wallets. The objective is to conceal the

Table 6.2 Mixers used by major blockchains

Blockchain	Mixer	Type	Status	Source
Ethereum	Tornado Cash, Railgun, Cyclone, Buccaneer V3, Messier 87	Decentralised	Active/sanctioned	Elliptic[a]
BSC	BNB Mixer, DDMixer, Cyclone fork	Custodial + decentralised	Active limited	GitHub
Polygon	Railgun, Cyclone, Messier 87 fork	Decentralised	Partially Inactive	Elliptic
Arbitrum	Tornado Cash (deploy), Railgun	Decentralised	Active	Cryptonews
Solana	Lava Cash, AINTI/Solmixer, NullTrace	Decentralised	Experimental	SmartLiquidity

[a]https://www.elliptic.com

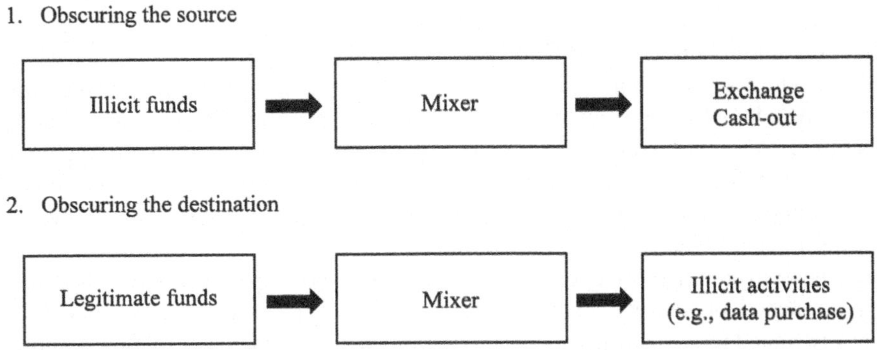

Fig. 6.2 Main recycling techniques

original source of the assets and disrupt forensic tracing prior to cash-out or conversion. The second is destination obfuscation, which operates in the opposite direction. In this case, funds are first withdrawn from an exchange and subsequently channelled through a mixer or private wallet infrastructure before being used to finance illicit activities. In both cases, the common effect is to weaken transaction-level traceability and delay attribution, thereby reducing the effectiveness of ex-post investigative and recovery efforts. The widespread use of mixers has materially reduced the probability of recovering stolen assets.

This dynamic illustrates a structural constraint of ex-post enforcement in pseudonymous blockchain environments. Once illicit proceeds enter a sufficiently large and active mixing pool, especially one operating across multiple chains or incorporating privacy enhancing cryptography, the cost and complexity of forensic reconstruction increase substantially, often rendering recovery economically or technically unfeasible.

In response to these challenges, authorities have adopted a range of countermeasures. The U.S. Office of Foreign Assets Control (OFAC) imposed sanctions on Tornado Cash and Blender.io, designating specific smart contracts and associated addresses in an effort to restrict their use by regulated entities. These measures aim to isolate mixers from the formal financial system by prohibiting interaction by compliant intermediaries. At the operational level, law enforcement actions have targeted infrastructure and custodial operators: the dismantling of ChipMixer by Europol in 2023 represents a significant example of coordinated cross-border intervention against a centralised mixing service. Parallel efforts have focused on enhancing technical investigative capabilities. Advances in blockchain analytics and de-anonymisation techniques have enabled selective successes in asset recovery, such as the retrieval of approximately USD 30 million linked to the Ronin bridge exploit.[3] These cases demonstrate that enforcement is not entirely ineffective.

[3] Back to Building: Ronin Security Breach Postmortem at: https://roninchain.com/blog/posts/back-to-building-ronin-security-breach-6513cc78a5edc1001b03c364.

6.2 Case Study: The Hack Ronin Bridge

In recent years, one of the most alarming developments in crypto-related crime has been the sharp increase in funds stolen from DeFi protocols, with cross-chain bridges emerging as particularly vulnerable targets. A substantial share of these illicit flows has been attributed to actors linked to North Korea, notably sophisticated groups such as the Lazarus Group. Estimates suggest that, in 2022 alone, North Korean-affiliated entities appropriated approximately USD 1.1 billion in cryptocurrency from DeFi platforms. As of mid-2022, cumulative losses from bridge-related exploits have been estimated at around USD 2 billion, underscoring the systemic relevance of this attack vector.[4]

Cross-chain bridges present an attractive target for several structural reasons. First, they often concentrate significant amounts of value within a limited number of smart contracts, effectively creating high-value honeypots. Second, their architecture is inherently complex: bridges typically involve on-chain components deployed on at least two distinct blockchains, combined with off-chain communication and validation mechanisms. This multi-layered structure expands the attack surface and increases the number of potential failure points, including validator compromise, message verification flaws, and governance weaknesses.

The attack on the Ronin Bridge, linked to the blockchain game Axie Infinity, remains the most prominent example.

On 23 March 2022, approximately $625 million was illicitly extracted, making it one of the largest crypto thefts to date. Ronin was designed as a dedicated sidechain to Ethereum, intended to facilitate faster and cheaper in-game transactions. The Ronin Bridge enabled users to transfer assets such as ETH and USDC between Ethereum and the Ronin sidechain, thereby supporting the purchase of NFTs and in-game tokens. The bridge operated under a trusted validator model. Transaction approvals required signatures from at least five out of nine designated validator nodes. However, the majority of these validators were controlled by Sky Mavis, the company behind Axie Infinity and Ronin, while another was operated by Axie DAO. This concentration of validation power significantly weakened the intended decentralisation of the system. The Lazarus Group succeeded in compromising the private keys of five validators, four belonging to Sky Mavis and one associated with Axie DAO. The breach of the Axie DAO validator stemmed from a prior operational arrangement: Sky Mavis had obtained permission from Axie DAO to sign transactions on its behalf via a gas-free RPC node. This delegated access was never revoked. Once the attackers infiltrated Sky Mavis' internal systems, they were able to exploit this residual authorization and secure the fifth required signature.

With control over five validator keys, the attackers effectively gained the ability to authorize fraudulent withdrawals. They subsequently transferred 173,600 ETH and 25.5 million USDC, amounting to roughly USD 625 million at the time of the exploit. The laundering phase that followed was highly fragmented, involving more

[4] Data from Chainanalysis: https://www.chainalysis.com/.

than 12,000 distinct blockchain addresses, further complicating tracing and recovery efforts.

The Ronin episode demonstrates how concentrated governance structures, deficiencies in operational controls, and architectural complexity can interact to generate systemic fragilities. It further underscores the geopolitical dimension of DeFi-related crime, as state-affiliated actors exploit structural weaknesses in decentralised infrastructures to extract and subsequently recycle substantial volumes of digital assets.

Figure 6.3 schematically illustrates a recurring laundering pattern attributed to North Korean-linked groups, structured around five sequential phases:

- First, the stolen Ether is distributed across a network of intermediary wallets, fragmenting the initial transaction trail.
- Second, the assets are channelled through Tornado Cash, where they are mixed in batches to disrupt traceability.
- Third, part of the Ether is converted into Bitcoin reportedly including approximately USD 20.5 million routed through Blender.io, a service later sanctioned by OFAC in 2022.
- Fourth, the acquired Bitcoin is itself subjected to additional batch-mixing operations, further increasing the opacity of the transactional chain.
- Fifth, the funds are transferred to crypto-to-fiat conversion platforms, where they can be monetised or withdrawn through conventional financial channels.

This multi-layered recycling process reflects a deliberate strategy aimed at combining fragmentation, cross-asset conversion, and jurisdictional dispersion to complicate enforcement efforts and maximise the probability of successful asset extraction.

The laundering strategy adopted by the Lazarus Group in the aftermath of the Ronin exploit illustrates the adaptive nature of crypto-enabled illicit finance. Initially, a significant portion of the stolen funds was routed through Tornado Cash, following

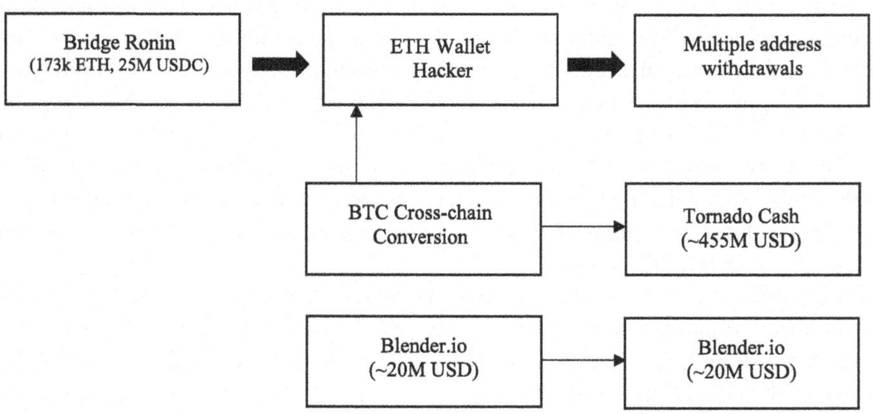

Fig. 6.3 DeFi recycling technique typically used in North Korea

a pattern consistent with previous large-scale exploits. However, after the U.S. Treasury's Office of Foreign Assets Control (OFAC) sanctioned Tornado Cash for facilitating the laundering of over USD 455 million linked to the Axie Infinity attack, the group progressively shifted away from this widely used Ethereum-based mixer. In response to increased scrutiny, Lazarus appears to have relied more extensively on decentralised finance infrastructures to conduct so-called *"chain hopping"*, a practice that involves transferring assets across multiple blockchains and converting them into different cryptocurrencies in rapid succession. While cross-chain bridges and asset swaps are predominantly used for legitimate interoperability and liquidity purposes, they can also be exploited to fragment transactional trails and complicate forensic analysis. By repeatedly moving assets between chains and altering their token form, actors can reduce the clarity of transaction linkages and increase the analytical burden on investigators.

As documented by Chainalysis, one observed chain-hopping sequence proceeds in three rapid steps within a short time window. First, funds are bridged from the Ethereum network to the BNB Chain (23 August 2022, 04:26 UTC). Second, the bridged assets are swapped from ETH into USDD on BNB Chain (23 August 2022, 05:17 UTC). Third, the resulting USDD is bridged onwards to the BitTorrent Chain (BTTC) (23 August 2022, 05:26 UTC). The transaction path involves a target address and an intermediary address, thereby inserting an additional layer between the initial chain and the final destination. In operational terms, this illustrates how cross-chain transfers and token conversions can be combined to fragment transactional trails and increase the analytical burden of attribution and tracing.

In sum, the Ronin Bridge exploit reveals both the operational sophistication of the Lazarus Group and the structural weaknesses embedded in the security architecture of the protocol at the time of the attack. The subsequent laundering phase, fragmented across thousands of blockchain addresses and multiple networks, reflects a high degree of coordination and strategic planning. The progressive shift toward complex techniques such as chain hopping, particularly following the sanctions imposed on Tornado Cash, illustrates the rapid adaptive capacity of organised crypto-criminal networks.

These developments show how illicit actors adjust their operational models in response to regulatory interventions, repurposing tools originally designed for interoperability or privacy into instruments of obfuscation and capital recycling. The case therefore highlights the limits of isolated enforcement measures and the need for a more systemic approach to risk mitigation. Strengthened security governance, clearer allocation of operational responsibilities, improved transparency in validator and bridge architectures, and enhanced cross-border cooperation, both among protocols and between industry and regulatory authorities, are essential components of an effective response to money laundering and the illicit exploitation of blockchain infrastructures (Belenkov et al., 2025).

In addition, the Ronin Bridge exploit is an illustrative case that intersects multiple risk categories within the proposed DeFi taxonomy. It simultaneously embodies governance risk, due to the concentration of validator control and the effective erosion of decentralisation, operational risk, arising from key management failures and inadequate internal controls, and, systemic interconnection risk, given the bridge's infrastructural role in linking distinct blockchain environments and concentrating large volumes of transferable value. Moreover, the subsequent laundering phase highlights conduct and illicit-finance amplification risks, whereby interoperable DeFi infrastructures are repurposed to facilitate large-scale obfuscation and capital recycling. The case is therefore analytically relevant because it demonstrates how different layers of risk, technical, organisational, financial, and geopolitical, can converge within a single protocol architecture. In this sense, Ronin serves as a clear example of how vulnerabilities in governance design and infrastructural concentration may evolve into systemic events with cross-chain and cross-jurisdictional implications, fully consistent with the multidimensional risk framework developed in Chapter 5.

From a macroprudential perspective, the Ronin case highlights how infrastructures originally designed to enhance interoperability can become potential vectors of systemic vulnerability once they reach sufficient scale and centrality. Cross-chain bridges operate as connective tissue within the DeFi ecosystem, linking liquidity pools, collateral structures, and user flows across networks. When such nodes concentrate large volumes of value and depend on governance or validation mechanisms that are only nominally decentralised, their failure does not remain confined to a single protocol. Instead, it may trigger broader effects through asset price adjustments, collateral liquidations, confidence shocks, and disruptions in cross-chain settlement.

Although, at present, DeFi and traditional finance remain only partially interconnected, the progressive integration of institutional actors, tokenised real-world assets, and regulated intermediaries could amplify the systemic relevance of similar events in the future. In this evolving environment, the stability of key infrastructural components, bridges, custodial validators, liquidity hubs, acquires macrofinancial significance. The Ronin exploit therefore anticipates a broader supervisory challenge: as DeFi architectures mature and scale, safeguarding financial stability will require not only micro-level security enhancements but also macro-level monitoring of infrastructural concentration, governance centralisation, and cross-network interdependencies.

References

Belenkov, N., Callens, V., Murashkin, A., Bak, K., Derka, M., Gorzny, J., & Lee, S.-S. (2025). *SoK: A review of cross-chain bridge hacks in 2023.* https://arxiv.org/abs/2501.03423

Tippe, P., & Deckers, C. (2025). Unmixing the mix: Patterns and challenges in Bitcoin mixer investigations. *Forensic Science International: Digital Investigation, 53*, Article 301876.

Chapter 7
Implications and Policy Recommendations

Abstract The redistribution of intermediation across decentralized architectures carries significant regulatory and policy implications. Institution-centered supervisory paradigms confront inherent limitations when applied to systems in which accountability is diffused across code, governance tokens, and infrastructural layers. This chapter formulates recommendations addressing reserve transparency, cross-jurisdictional coordination, governance design, and data standardization. Rather than advocating prescriptive uniformity, it argues for adaptive oversight mechanisms calibrated to the structural properties of decentralized financial arrangements.

* * *

7.1 Stakeholder Implications and Mitigation Strategies

In light of the incidents data and the proposed taxonomy, it is clear that a multi-level approach is necessary to identify risks early and mitigate their impact. Below, we outline key implications for various stakeholders in the DeFi ecosystem-users/investors, developers/protocols, market participants-and propose strategies consistent with emerging practices, supporting them with quantitative metrics where possible.

7.1.1 Continuous Monitoring and Data Analytics (for Protocols and Analysts)

Given how quickly exploits can occur, it is crucial to implement real-time on-chain activity surveillance systems to detect anomalies. Protocol teams and security firms should use algorithms that track early indicators of attack, such as abnormal fund movements (sudden massive exits from a liquidity pool; increasing token concentration in a few wallets); suspicious DEX trading patterns (volume spikes or volatility

L. Barbaro et al., *Crypto and Decentralized Finance Under Stress*,
SpringerBriefs in Finance, https://doi.org/10.1007/978-3-032-28425-9_7

on otherwise illiquid pairs); and unexpected use of flash loans in protocols where they don't normally appear. These signals can anticipate a possible ongoing hack or imminent rugpull. For example, using flash loans combined with operations on low-liquid assets could signal an attempt at price manipulation; a sudden shift of all tokens in a project to service addresses (e.g., mixers) could indicate that founders are performing an exit scam. In this sense, MEV bots can also act as both a threat and an indicator: repetitive transactions with very high gas to anticipate orders on DEXs suggest the presence of aggressive front-runners, a sign of possible arbitrage or manipulation opportunities taking place.

Supervisors and analytics providers are starting to develop dedicated dashboards: in the US, for example, the Treasury Department has emphasized the need to invest in tools for monitoring illicit risks in DeFi and sharing public–private information on emerging threats (FSB, 2023; Daian et al., 2019). A known challenge is the scarcity of reliable and comparable data: IOSCO highlights significant information gaps in the DeFi ecosystem (pseudonym transactions, difficulty distinguishing retail vs. institutional users, etc.) (Makarov et al., 2022). Improving data collection appears necessary to strengthen risk monitoring capacity. This can be done by requiring major protocols to publish periodic metrics and audits of reserves, liquidity, and uses, as well as by promoting common on-chain reporting standards (e.g., smart contracts that expose key risk data via APIs). This increased transparency would help both regulators and advanced users identify risk situations before they escalate.

7.1.2 Identifying Managers and Transparency in Governance (for Project Teams and Communities)

A unique problem with DeFi is the difficulty of identifying responsible parties to whom regulatory obligations or corrective actions can be attributed, given that many protocols claim to be "decentralized" and without leadership. There are core developers and sometimes legal entities (e.g. foundations) behind each project. IOSCO recommends that authorities require DeFi projects to clearly state roles and responsibilities behind protocols, even when formally decentralized (Werbach, 2018).

While awaiting regulatory requirements, it is in the protocols' interest to improve trust by transparently communicating their governance: for example, maintaining public records of core developers, validators, or core node operators, and documenting on-chain decision-making processes (who proposes and votes on changes). More transparent governance open to public scrutiny helps mitigate operational risks and conflicts of interest. If a protocol communicates a critical change to risk parameters (collateral factor, yield) in advance, users can react and report any critical issues before implementation. Many DeFi projects have introduced security mechanisms into governance, such as quorum requirements and minimum voting times to avoid hasty decisions, or the establishment of security committees with limited powers to pause smart contracts in the event of a full-blown exploit.

It is important for community stakeholders to support such measures and demand high standards of effective decentralization: for example, preferring protocols with distributed multisigs and timelocks for updates, avoiding projects where a developer controls administrative keys alone. Future empirical studies may confirm that protocols with more decentralized and transparent governance suffer fewer incidents.

7.1.3 Improving Technological Resilience (for Developers and Auditors)

From a technical perspective, there are several strategies for mitigating exploit risks. A well-established best practice is to conduct independent code audits: having smart contract code reviewed by third-party security companies can identify common vulnerabilities before launch. However, as previously discussed, audits do not guarantee full coverage, especially when faced with new financial logic or additions with external oracles. For protocols that handle large sums or critical functions, the use of formal checks (mathematical proofs of code correctness) would be desirable at least for the most sensitive modules, for instance, collateral management contracts or Net Asset Value calculations of algorithmic stablecoins.

Regulators and institutional investors may in the future demand security certifications as a prerequisite for interacting with certain protocols (similar to how banks and funds today require IT audit certificates from suppliers). For example, the EU with MiCA will require significant token issuers and crypto service providers to take steps to ensure risk-proportioned cybersecurity. Alongside audits, it is crucial to incentivize responsible bug discovery: bug bounty programs like Immunefi[1] have already helped prevent serious vulnerabilities by rewarding hackers "white hat". In parallel, the DeFi community could benefit from the creation of a sort of "Underwriters Laboratory" for smart contracts, which is an independent body that conducts standardized robustness tests on widely used contracts (e.g., ERC-20 templates, AMM implementations, lending modules) and publishes a security rating. This would provide a public and unbiased reference on the quality of projects' code, helping users distinguish well-built protocols from improvised and potentially insecure forks.

Finally, on the protocol side, it is advisable to implement algorithmic limitations and emergencies: for example, circuit breakers or automatic limits that trigger in the event of anomalous conditions (liquidity drying, price excursions > X%, etc.), temporarily freezing some operations. Some large DeFi protocols have begun to integrate these logics (e.g. Aave has daily borrow limits for risky assets). Such measures add a layer of security, although they introduce latency and temporary "centralization", a trade-off necessary in the face of lightning threats.

---

[1] Immunefi Team. (2024) Exploit analyses, available at: https://immunefi.com/research/.

7.1.4 Investor Education and Tools

DeFi users, especially retail and institutional users, face a higher level of risk and complexity than traditional finance. It is therefore essential to strengthen financial and digital education initiatives focused on crypto and DeFi: investors should be aware of the main scam schemes (rugpull, phishing, etc.) and the warning signs to observe before interacting with a protocol. Some red flags empirically associated with fraudulent projects include: promises of extremely high returns compared to the market average (e.g., pools offering > 1000% APY on common assets—often a prelude to Ponzi schemes) (Chen et al., 2020); lack of open-source code or public audits; totally anonymous and/or unverified teams; tokenomics that allocate a huge share of tokens to the team/founders; deposit locking mechanisms that are too restrictive or unclear. Investors should diversify and never allocate more than they are willing to lose into individual high-risk DeFi protocols. For institutional or professional investors entering DeFi, it is advisable to adopt a risk-management approach: use on-chain analytics tools to monitor a protocol's health indicators in real time (TVL, collateral usage, default rates, abnormal activity), use protocol rating services (some startups are starting to offer them), and demand clear contractual conditions (for example, preferring protocols with integrated insurance, or with circuit breaker[2] clauses as above). In the future, standard metrics (e.g., DeFi Sharpe ratio) could emerge to compare risk/return on DeFi strategies, or protocol solvency scores calculated by third parties. This would greatly help users navigate the landscape.

7.1.5 Risk Insurance and Mutualization

A growing mitigation mechanism is decentralized hacks insurance. There are protocols (Nexus Mutual, InsurAce, etc.) that offer coverage by compensating users in the event of a loss of funds due to smart contract exploits or bugs. These solutions replicate the traditional insurance function: capital pools collect premiums from policyholders and pay claims when covered hacks occur, with patterns ranging from mutualistic to parametric insurance (e.g., policies that pay if a stablecoin loses its peg beyond certain percentage points). Adopting insurance can reduce the final impact for affected investors and indirectly incentivize virtuous behaviour (companies often require audits and minimum standards from the protocol to be insured, acting as certifiers). Currently, penetration of these tools remains limited compared to the overall DeFi market, partly due to insufficient insurance capital to cover a systemic collapse.

Policy initiatives could be envisaged to strengthen this layer of risk absorption. Tax or regulatory incentives might encourage DeFi operators to obtain coverage or contribute to sector-specific mutual funds. A useful analogy can be drawn with traditional financial infrastructures, where clearing or guarantee funds (e.g., interbank

[2] The circuit breaker is an emergency mechanism that temporarily suspends the operations of a protocol or market in the presence of serious anomalies, such as extreme volatility or attacks.

deposit protection schemes) provide collective backstops. Of course, in the absence of a regulatory obligation, such voluntary mechanisms risk being underfunded (adverse selection problem). However, bodies such as the BIS have suggested the idea of incorporating prudential rules directly into protocols ("embedding supervision in code") and setting up backstops for critical functions such as stablecoins (Bank of England, 2022).

Looking ahead, it is not out of the question that central banks or public consortia could provide last-resort liquidity facilities for segments of the crypto market (e.g., systemic stablecoins), provided that such protocols adhere to rigorous security standards-an analogy to the lender of last resort role in the banking system. We are probably far from that, but meanwhile risk mutualisation through decentralised insurance remains a promising and evolving tool.

The strategies described above highlight that no single measure is decisive: a coordinated set of technological solutions, market measures, and user precautions is needed to effectively mitigate DeFi risks. For example, the widespread adoption of audits and bug bounties[3] may reduce common technical exploits, but it will not eliminate the risks of fraudulent conduct; similarly, sophisticated on-chain monitoring systems may detect ongoing attacks, but it is still necessary to prevent funds from flowing indiscriminately to untrustworthy projects (education and disclosure issues). Ultimately, all ecosystem players-developers, users, crypto intermediaries, authorities-have shared responsibilities in building a more secure and resilient DeFi environment.

7.2 Regulatory and Policy Recommendations

Supervisory authorities worldwide are increasingly confronted with the challenge of integrating DeFi within established standards of financial security and market integrity, while avoiding regulatory responses that might unnecessarily constrain technological innovation. In this context, IOSCO (2023) has articulated nine high-level recommendations aimed at framing a coherent regulatory approach to DeFi. A central pillar of this framework is an activity-based approach grounded in the principle of technological neutrality. Regulators are encouraged to analyse DeFi products and services according to their economic function and risk profile, rather than their technological form, in line with the maxim "*same activity, same risk, same regulatory outcome*". Under this logic, blockchain-based arrangements that replicate traditional activities such as deposit-taking, credit intermediation, or collective investment management, should, where appropriate, be subject to regulatory obligations comparable to those applicable in traditional finance. A related objective concerns the containment of regulatory arbitrage. DeFi should not evolve into a

[3] Bug bounty is an incentive program that offers financial rewards to developers or security researchers who identify and report vulnerabilities in the code of a protocol or smart contract before they can be exploited.

regulatory vacuum exploited to circumvent existing legal standards. Where decentralised architectures replicate the features of regulated financial instruments such as derivatives or portfolio management services, existing laws should be applied, and legal responsibility should be attached to identifiable economic actors involved in the design, governance, or operation of the protocol (Werbach, 2018). Several jurisdictions are therefore exploring mechanisms to attribute accountability to developers, core teams, or key holders behind ostensibly decentralised systems, with a view to ensuring enforceability of anti-fraud, market abuse, and investor protection rules.

Transparency and disclosure requirements constitute another essential dimension. Reducing information asymmetries, particularly for retail users, requires DeFi projects to provide clear and comprehensive disclosures regarding governance structures, audit status of smart contracts, embedded risks, and potential conflicts of interest (Werbach, 2018). In practice, this could entail the introduction of standardised risk warnings within protocol interfaces, including explicit statements on the absence of deposit insurance or the presence of unaudited code, mirroring disclosure practices common in traditional financial markets. Given the inherently cross-border nature of DeFi, effective supervision also depends on enhanced international cooperation. Coordinated enforcement actions, intelligence sharing on fraud and scams, and convergence toward common regulatory standards are necessary to prevent malicious actors from relocating to more permissive jurisdictions. International bodies such as the FSB and IOSCO are promoting such coordination, but meaningful implementation ultimately depends on the commitment and legislative action of individual countries.

A concrete regulatory development is the European MiCAR (Markets in Cryptoassets) regulation, approved in 2023, which introduces uniform rules for cryptoasset issuance and services in the EU. MiCAR specifically covers stablecoins (distinguishing between asset-referenced tokens and e-money tokens) and various services such as trading, custody, and cryptoasset consulting (European Union, 2023). However, MiCAR explicitly excludes from its perimeter truly decentralized activities without identifiable intermediaries (for example, totally permissionless token issuance). This leaves a regulatory grey area: many DeFi applications will initially escape the MiCAR regime until there is an identifiable legal entity "promoter" or service provider. For example, a pure AMM with no parent company does not fall under MiCAR; however, if a centralized exchange offers access to tokens generated by that AMM, it may have to comply with transparency requirements for those tokens. ESMA has indicated that it will issue guidelines on aspects such as cryptoasset staking, DeFi lending, etc., to bridge some gaps in the meantime. Looking ahead, a MiCAR 2.0 that explicitly addresses DeFi is possible, but in the meantime, it will be crucial to encourage forms of self-regulation in the industry: independent audits, proof-of-reserves, and public on-chain asset registries are all practices that industry can voluntarily adopt to demonstrate reliability and cooperate with regulators.

Another area of regulatory focus is stablecoins and stores of value in the DeFi system. The collapse of TerraUSD demonstrated the potential systemic impact of an unsecured algorithmic stablecoins. MiCAR already has stringent requirements for significant stablecoins (in terms of capital, reserves, mandatory audits) but only if there is an identified central issuer. For decentralized stablecoins or algorithms, ad hoc interventions or inclusion in future regulatory packages will likely be needed. Some experts propose the idea of certifying stablecoins algorithms or placing limits on the allowed algorithmic leverage (e.g., requiring minimal collateralization). Furthermore, the possibility of integrating security "guardrails" at the protocol level is discussed: the BIS suggested that some prudential controls could be directly encoded in smart contracts (e.g., self-regulating risk parameters) to prevent certain ex ante excessively risky behaviors (Makarov et al., 2022; Werbach, 2018).

On the enforcement side, authorities are stepping up efforts to prosecute crypto crimes. Coordinated action, as against the Lazarus Group (see Chapter 6), indicates that large-scale DeFi attacks are now considered a threat to international security. Financial cybercrime units specializing in blockchain must therefore be strengthened, promoting collaboration between agencies (law enforcement, financial intelligence) and with private actors (exchanges that can freeze stolen funds, analytics firms that track flows). The goal is to make the risk of legal consequences more tangible even for hackers operating through DeFi. In parallel, the adequacy of the existing regulatory framework needs to be assessed: for example, anti-money laundering legislation will likely need to extend to include DEXs and smart contracts in some way, perhaps requiring front-ends or aggregators to integrate AML controls for access to certain services.

Ultimately, the regulatory recommendations converge on several key points: filling the regulatory gap by applying existing laws to DeFi where possible; imposing principles of prudence and transparency (disclosures, conflict management, audit requirements) similar to those in the financial sector; and promoting international convergence to avoid arbitrage. Authorities must, however, balance intervention with the need to avoid stifling innovation: overregulation could push DeFi operations completely into the shadows or into unregulated platforms abroad, increasing rather than reducing systemic risks. One desired path is to co-create solutions: involving the DeFi community in setting standards (e.g., certifications, security best practices) and possibly providing regulatory sandboxes where new on-chain compliance models can be tested (such as embedded supervision projects that use smart contracts to automate regulatory reporting).

References

Bank of England. (2022). *Cryptoassets and decentralised finance: Financial stability in focus*. https://www.bankofengland.co.uk/financial-stability-in-focus/2022/march-2022

Chen, Y., & Bellavitis, C. (2020). Blockchain disruption and decentralized finance: The rise of decentralized business models. *Journal of Business Venturing Insights, 13*, Article e00151.

Daian, P., Goldfeder, S., Bentov, I., Kell, T., Breidenbach, L., Li, Y., Zhao, X., & Juels, A. (2019). Flash boys 2.0: Frontrunning, transaction reordering, and consensus instability in decentralized exchanges. *arXiv*. https://arxiv.org/abs/1904.05234.

European Union. (2023). Regulation (EU) 2023/1114 of the European Parliament and of the Council of 31 May 2023 on markets in crypto-assets, and amending Regulations (EU) No 1093/2010 and

(EU) No 1095/2010 and Directives 2013/36/EU and (EU) 2019/1937. *Official Journal of the European Union, L 150*, 1–130. https://eurlex.europa.eu/legal-content/EN/TXT/?uri=CELEX:32023R1114

International Organization of Securities Commissions (IOSCO). (2023). *Policy recommendations for decentralized finance (DeFi)*

Makarov, I., & Schoar, A. (2022). *Cryptocurrencies and decentralized finance (DeFi)*. NBER working paper no. 30006. National Bureau of Economic Research. https://www.nber.org/papers/w30006

Werbach, K. (2018). *The blockchain and the new architecture of trust*. MIT Press.

Closing Remarks

The analysis conducted highlighted how decentralized finance represents both an opportunity for innovation and a source of significant risks to the stability and integrity of the financial system. The proposed updated taxonomy allowed us to more precisely distinguish the different types of vulnerabilities, from market and credit risks to operational, governance, and systemic risks, showing how they intertwine in a highly interconnected and rapidly evolving ecosystem. Empirical data confirm the coexistence of two complementary dynamics: on the one hand, a multitude of small but recurring incidents, often linked to widespread fraud and minor technical vulnerabilities; on the other, a smaller number of exceptional events, characterized by catastrophic losses and potential systemic contagion effects. This asymmetry requires differentiated mitigation approaches: widespread protection of retail investors against small-scale scams, but also macroprudential and regulatory tools to prevent and contain systemic risks.

A further critical element that has emerged concerns the ambivalent role of mixers and other pseudo-anonymous infrastructures, which, while responding to legitimate privacy needs, today constitute a privileged channel for laundering illicit proceeds, drastically reducing the possibility of recovering stolen funds. This makes strengthening international cooperation, adopting advanced on-chain tracking techniques, and developing innovative regulatory tools that balance security and confidentiality protection essential.

DeFi does not eliminate financial risk. It reconfigures its sources, transmission channels, and accountability structures. Understanding this reconfiguration is the precondition for designing proportionate, technologically informed, and forward-looking regulatory responses. In conclusion, the evolution of DeFi poses unprecedented challenges for policymakers, investors, and market participants. Only an integrated approach, combining technology surveillance, risk management strategies, more transparent governance mechanisms and a globally harmonised regulatory framework, can make it possible to leverage the benefits of innovation without compromising financial stability and user confidence. The ability to successfully

L. Barbaro et al., *Crypto and Decentralized Finance Under Stress*, SpringerBriefs in Finance, https://doi.org/10.1007/978-3-032-28425-9

address such challenges will determine not only the resilience of the DeFi sector, but also its degree of legitimization and integration into the international financial architecture of the future.

Appendix A: Attack Methods

This section presents the complete dataset of attack methods used in DeFi between 2016 and 2025 as documented by the DefiLlama platform. Furthermore, the definition of each attack technique is reported.

Method	Incidents (N)	Share of incidents (%)	Total loss (USD mln)	Share of total loss (%)	Average loss per incident (USD mln)
Private key compromised (unknown method)	44	11.46	2985.441	25.52	67.851
Safe multisig wallet phishing exploit	2	0.52	1634.900	13.97	817.450
Access control exploit	18	4.69	752.489	6.43	41.805
Private key compromised (social engineering)	4	1.04	631.820	5.40	157.955
Proof verifier bug	1	0.26	570.000	4.87	570.000
Flashloan price oracle attack	28	7.29	424.070	3.62	15.145
Signature exploit	2	0.52	407.700	3.48	203.850
Flashloan donate function logic exploit	5	1.30	228.100	1.95	45.620
Spoof token exploit	1	0.26	223.000	1.91	223.000
Math mistake exploit	4	1.04	215.750	1.84	53.938
Database attack	1	0.26	200.000	1.71	200.000
Trusted root exploit	1	0.26	190.000	1.62	190.000
Flashloan governance attack	1	0.26	181.000	1.55	181.000
Flashloan reentrancy attack	17	4.43	179.090	1.53	10.535

(continued)

L. Barbaro et al., *Crypto and Decentralized Finance Under Stress*, SpringerBriefs in Finance, https://doi.org/10.1007/978-3-032-28425-9

(continued)

Method	Incidents (N)	Share of incidents (%)	Total loss (USD mln)	Share of total loss (%)	Average loss per incident (USD mln)
Price oracle attack	10	2.60	176.479	1.51	17.648
Hot wallet hack	4	1.04	162.200	1.39	40.550
Private key compromised (brute force)	2	0.52	160.865	1.37	80.433
Reentrancy	19	4.95	154.250	1.32	8.118
Drained contracts	13	3.39	152.320	1.30	11.717
Contract not initialized	1	0.26	150.000	1.28	150.000
Cloudflare key compromised	4	1.04	131.815	1.13	32.954
Private key compromised	6	1.56	114.105	0.98	19.017
Transfer logic exploit	2	0.52	101.000	0.86	50.500
Market-making bot exploit	1	0.26	100.000	0.85	100.000
Duplicate call exploit	1	0.26	90.000	0.77	90.000
Infinite mint and dump	7	1.82	68.800	0.59	9.829
Flashloan pool shares exploit	5	1.30	68.757	0.59	13.751
Storage slot exploit	1	0.26	62.500	0.53	62.500
Vyper compiler bug	1	0.26	61.700	0.53	61.700
Private key compromised (phishing)	2	0.52	59.300	0.51	29.650
Flashloan swap logic exploit	2	0.52	59.000	0.50	29.500
Drained liquidity pool	3	0.78	51.900	0.44	17.300
Dev privilege oversight exploit	1	0.26	49.500	0.42	49.500
Collateral validation exploit	1	0.26	48.000	0.41	48.000
Claim contract flashloan exploit	1	0.26	44.700	0.38	44.700
Price oracle manipulation	5	1.30	39.000	0.33	7.800
Social engineering	2	0.52	37.420	0.32	18.710
Swap function exploit	1	0.26	31.400	0.27	31.400
Private key compromised (stored publicly)	3	0.78	27.800	0.24	9.267
Cross chain multisig deployment exploit	1	0.26	27.600	0.24	27.600

(continued)

(continued)

Method	Incidents (N)	Share of incidents (%)	Total loss (USD mln)	Share of total loss (%)	Average loss per incident (USD mln)
Drained contracts and user wallets	1	0.26	27.000	0.23	27.000
API key unauthorized access	1	0.26	26.000	0.22	26.000
Outdated oracle exploit	3	0.78	25.400	0.22	8.467
Flashloan incentive rewards exploit	5	1.30	25.085	0.21	5.017
Delegatecall exploit	2	0.52	22.950	0.20	11.475
Vault swap exploit	1	0.26	19.700	0.17	19.700
Borrow logic exploit	3	0.78	18.000	0.15	6.000
Flashloan withdraw logic exploit	1	0.26	18.000	0.15	18.000
Private key compromised (malware)	3	0.78	16.300	0.14	5.433
Voting power inflation	1	0.26	16.000	0.14	16.000
Price manipulation attack	4	1.04	15.900	0.14	3.975
Migrate function mistake exploit	1	0.26	15.800	0.14	15.800
Log spoofing	1	0.26	13.000	0.11	13.000
MEV bot manipulation exploit	1	0.26	12.000	0.10	12.000
Flashloan trove manipulation	1	0.26	11.600	0.10	11.600
Flashloan misconfiguration exploit	1	0.26	11.539	0.10	11.539
Incentives function mistake	2	0.52	11.000	0.09	5.500
Frontend attack	3	0.78	9.938	0.08	3.313
Deposit function exploit	2	0.52	9.800	0.08	4.900
Router exploit via infinite approvals	1	0.26	9.730	0.08	9.730
Empty market exploit	1	0.26	9.550	0.08	9.550
Oracle manipulation	2	0.52	9.370	0.08	4.685
Private key compromised (supply chain attack)	2	0.52	8.720	0.07	4.360
CTX exploit	1	0.26	8.700	0.07	8.700
Malicious transfer() method	1	0.26	8.373	0.07	8.373
Refund logic exploit	1	0.26	8.000	0.07	8.000

(continued)

(continued)

Method	Incidents (N)	Share of incidents (%)	Total loss (USD mln)	Share of total loss (%)	Average loss per incident (USD mln)
Private key compromised (bad ECDSA implementation)	1	0.26	7.900	0.07	7.900
Flashloan slippage attack	2	0.52	7.850	0.07	3.925
DebtManager exploit	1	0.26	7.200	0.06	7.200
Token approval exploit	2	0.52	7.140	0.06	3.570
Missing input validation	3	0.78	6.810	0.06	2.270
Fee overflow exploit	1	0.26	6.800	0.06	6.800
Burn function mistake	1	0.26	6.500	0.06	6.500
Collateral offboarding mistake	1	0.26	6.000	0.05	6.000
Malicious governance proposal	1	0.26	6.000	0.05	6.000
Acces control exploit	3	0.78	5.786	0.05	1.929
Flashloan exploit	4	1.04	5.630	0.05	1.407
Calldata underflow and resolver hijack	1	0.26	5.000	0.04	5.000
IBC hooks exploit	1	0.26	5.000	0.04	5.000
Guardian 2FA service exploit	1	0.26	5.000	0.04	5.000
Over-ride logic exploit	1	0.26	5.000	0.04	5.000
Debt swap exploit	1	0.26	4.800	0.04	4.800
Flashloan new market exploit	2	0.52	4.750	0.04	2.375
Misconfiguration	1	0.26	4.589	0.04	4.589
Flashloan burn function exploit	1	0.26	4.500	0.04	4.500
Exploit weak authentication check	1	0.26	4.400	0.04	4.400
Fake collateral exploit	1	0.26	4.000	0.03	4.000
Liquidation logic exploit	1	0.26	4.000	0.03	4.000
Drain vaults	2	0.52	3.850	0.03	1.925
Router exploit	3	0.78	3.399	0.03	1.133
Redirected deposits	1	0.26	3.100	0.03	3.100
Governance and oracle exploit	1	0.26	3.000	0.03	3.000
Front-end vulnerability	1	0.26	3.000	0.03	3.000
Arbitrary external call	3	0.78	2.765	0.02	0.922

(continued)

(continued)

Method	Incidents (N)	Share of incidents (%)	Total loss (USD mln)	Share of total loss (%)	Average loss per incident (USD mln)
DNS spoofing	2	0.52	2.575	0.02	1.288
Exploit lack of input authentication	1	0.26	2.300	0.02	2.300
Missing condition check	1	0.26	2.260	0.02	2.260
Unknown	3	0.78	2.203	0.02	0.734
Decimal miscalculation exploit	1	0.26	2.160	0.02	2.160
External call vulnerability	1	0.26	2.100	0.02	2.100
Transferred treasury to mixers	1	0.26	2.100	0.02	2.100
Ownership override attack	2	0.52	1.975	0.02	0.988
Unvalidated call data exploit	1	0.26	1.960	0.02	1.960
Redeem function exploit	1	0.26	1.891	0.02	1.891
Referral claims logic exploit	2	0.52	1.815	0.02	0.907
User balances manually updated	1	0.26	1.750	0.01	1.750
Minting logic exploit	1	0.26	1.700	0.01	1.700
Storage misalignment exploit	1	0.26	1.600	0.01	1.600
Address poisoning	1	0.26	1.450	0.01	1.450
Buy function exploit	1	0.26	1.400	0.01	1.400
OverPaper function exploit	1	0.26	1.300	0.01	1.300
Private key compromised (discord hack)	1	0.26	1.270	0.01	1.270
Deployer wallet compromised	1	0.26	1.157	0.01	1.157
Inconsistent value in code	1	0.26	1.000	0.01	1.000
Donation attack	1	0.26	0.902	0.01	0.902
Inflationary accounting manipulation	1	0.26	0.900	0.01	0.900
Missing access control	1	0.26	0.900	0.01	0.900
Redeem rounding error exploit	2	0.52	0.750	0.01	0.375

(continued)

(continued)

Method	Incidents (N)	Share of incidents (%)	Total loss (USD mln)	Share of total loss (%)	Average loss per incident (USD mln)
Liquidity pools compromised	1	0.26	0.620	0.01	0.620
Incentive rewards exploit	2	0.52	0.578	0.00	0.289
fillQuote silo.borrow() Exploit	1	0.26	0.546	0.00	0.546
withdrawStuckToken() exploit	1	0.26	0.500	0.00	0.500
Staking logic exploit	1	0.26	0.500	0.00	0.500
Rounding donation attack	1	0.26	0.464	0.00	0.464
Oracle misconfiguration exploit	2	0.52	0.450	0.00	0.225
API signature exploit	1	0.26	0.450	0.00	0.450
Private key compromised (session signer)	1	0.26	0.400	0.00	0.400
Transient storage collision	1	0.26	0.355	0.00	0.355
Calculation error in liquidation engine	1	0.26	0.340	0.00	0.340
Unchecked FlashLoan approve exploit	1	0.26	0.300	0.00	0.300
Controlled rebalance manipulation	1	0.26	0.300	0.00	0.300
Withdraw function argument manipulation	1	0.26	0.228	0.00	0.228
Private key compromised (vanity address)	1	0.26	0.200	0.00	0.200
Bonding curve exploit	1	0.26	0.200	0.00	0.200
Redeem process exploit	1	0.26	0.198	0.00	0.198
Liquidity pool exploit	1	0.26	0.183	0.00	0.183
Balance disparity exploit	1	0.26	0.181	0.00	0.181
Unlimited repeated withdrawal exploit	1	0.26	0.094	0.00	0.094
Mint reserves logic exploit	1	0.26	0.090	0.00	0.090
Replay attack	1	0.26	0.068	0.00	0.068
Arbitration exploit	1	0.26	0.043	0.00	0.043
CEX price manipulation attack	1	0.26	0.037	0.00	0.037

(continued)

(continued)

Method	Incidents (N)	Share of incidents (%)	Total loss (USD mln)	Share of total loss (%)	Average loss per incident (USD mln)
Proxy upgrade skim	1	0.26	0.011	0.00	0.011
Others	10	2.60	67.700	0.58	6.770
Total	384	100.00	11,699.449	100.00	30.467

Attacks Definitions

Access Control Exploit: An exploit in which an attacker exploits incorrect or absent configurations in the access control mechanisms of a DeFi smart contract, gaining unauthorized privileges, modifying the contract state, or performing restricted functions, often due to a lack of Ownable, onlyOwner, require() modules, or poorly managed roles (Zhou et al., 2023).

Address Poisoning: A phishing attack that exploits the address shortening mechanism in Web3 platforms (e.g. Etherscan, MetaMask) to insert false addresses into the victim's transaction history, causing them to transfer funds to a malicious address very similar to a legitimate one (Guan et al., 2024).

API Key unauthorized access: An attack in which an attacker gains unauthorized access to the functionality of a wallet, smart contract, or DeFi infrastructure by exploiting an exposed, mishandled, or compromised API key (Li et al., 2022).

API Signature Exploit: An exploit that allows an attacker to generate valid API signatures without knowing the shared secret key, exploiting structural weaknesses in the signature algorithm (e.g. MD5), such as the length-extension attack (Duong et al., 2009).

Arbitrary External Call: A situation in which a software system (e.g., smart contract, control module, algorithm) makes calls to uncontrolled or unverified external components, introducing arbitrary noise, unpredictable behavior, or security vulnerabilities, similar to the concept of external arbitrary noise in the statistical model (Senov et al., 2014).

Arbitration Exploit: Malicious behavior that exploits economic arbitrage or protocol mechanisms in a manner not intended or authorized by the system, with the aim of obtaining unfair advantage, illicit profits, or market manipulation (Li et al., 2022).

Balance Disparity Exploit: An attack technique in which an individual exploits temporary or structural imbalances in the balance sheets of smart contracts or liquidity pools to gain unfair economic benefits, often bypassing the protection mechanisms provided by the protocol (Chen et al., 2023).

Bonding Curve Exploit: An attack technique that exploits vulnerabilities or asymmetries in the automated token pricing function, based on bonding curves, to generate unfair profit (Qian et al., 2023).

Borrow Logic Exploit: An attack technique in which a malicious actor exploits logical flaps in the lending process of a DeFi protocol, such as collateral management, checking loan terms, or interacting with smart contracts, to obtain assets unauthorizedly or unfairly (Qian et al., 2023).

Burn Function Mistake: A design or security flaw in a smart contract's burn() function that allows unauthorized destruction of tokens, or fails to properly update totalSupply, resulting in economic imbalances or vulnerabilities (Qian et al., 2023).

Buy Function Exploit: An attack that targets the buy() function of a DeFi contract, exploiting poorly formed inputs, lack of price controls, or insecure dependencies (e.g., oracles, rewards, external callbacks) to incorrectly obtain tokens at favorable conditions (Qian et al., 2023).

Calculation Error in Liquidation Engine: A logical, computational, or design error within the automated liquidation system of a DeFi protocol, leading to incorrect, unjustified, or missed liquidations.

Calldata underflow: An error that occurs when a contract receives less data than expected in the calldata structure, resulting in unexpected memory accesses, validation bypasses, or uninitialized variable reads (Shou et al., 2024).

CEX Price Manipulation Attack: A strategy in which an attacker temporarily manipulates the price of an asset on a centralized platform (CEX), knowing that that price data will be used by a DeFi protocol through an oracle, to obtain unfair profits or activate automated behaviors (liquidations, swaps, collateral updates) (Xiong et al., 2024).

Claim Contract Flashloan Exploit: An attack technique in which a malicious actor exploits the claim (request for rewards or benefits) function of a DeFi contract, temporarily manipulating the protocol state through a flash loan within a single transaction. This allows you to simulate artificial eligibility conditions, receive the expected reward, and restore the original state by returning the flash loan, bypassing contract controls (Wu, 2024).

Cloudflare Key Compromised: A security incident in which a private key (or critical token) managed through the Cloudflare infrastructure is exposed, stolen, or misused. This can compromise the integrity of the HTTPS connection, enable man-in-the-middle attacks, allow decryption of TLS traffic, or allow unauthorized access to systems dependent on that key (Bhargavan et al., 2017).

Collateral Offboarding Mistake: A logical, operational, or governance error in the removal (offboarding) process of a collateral asset supported by a DeFi protocol. It can cause forced devaluation, unintentional liquidation, or loss of funds by users who still hold positions based on such collateral (Aspris, 2025).

Collateral Validation Exploit: An attack that exploits weaknesses in the collateral verification (validation) logic in a DeFi protocol. When the smart contract does not adequately control the legitimacy, value, or provenance of the collateral deposited, an attacker can simulate valid assets to obtain undeserved loans, rewards, or privileges (Aspris, 2025).

Contract not initialized: A vulnerability condition that occurs when a smart contract is deployed on the blockchain without properly initializing critical variables, state structures, or external modules (such as proxies or oracle bindings) (Zhou et al., 2023).

Controlled Rebalance Manipulation: A form of attack in which an actor, through direct or indirect control of funds and wallets within a DeFi protocol with automated rebalancing mechanisms, artificially alters the distribution of assets in the pool, inducing fraudulent economic benefits such as positive slippage, fund drainage, or exchange price manipulation.

Cross Chain Multisig Deployment Exploit: An attack that targets multisig (multi-signature) protocols distributed across multiple blockchains, exploiting inconsistencies between security, quorum, and addressing configurations across different networks. It allows the attacker to bypass authorization checks, duplicate the signature on a different chain, or manipulate the signature logic in cross-chain environments (Harris, 2023).

CTX Exploit: Vulnerability that exploits inefficient or insecure handling of Cross-shard Transactions (CTXs) in fragmented (sharded) blockchain protocols. Attack occurs when an actor manipulates the selection, distribution, or confirmation of CTXs, often through incentivized brokers or rebalancing mechanisms, to extract value, bypass atomicity rules (Chen et al., 2024).

Database Attack: A category of exploits in which an attacker inserts or manipulates malicious code that is subsequently saved, interpreted, or executed within a database. These attacks may include SQL injection, second-order injection, or structural manipulations that compromise database integrity and security.

Debt Swap Exploit: A DeFi protocol attack strategy that leverages the settlement of undercollateralized loans using flashswaps, manipulating exchange rates between debt and collateral assets to achieve higher profits than conventional settlement strategies (Yaish et al., 2023).

DebtManager Exploit: An attack technique that exploits logical or design vulnerabilities in the debt management module ("Debt Manager") of a DeFi protocol. The attacker manipulates functions such as settlement, repayment, collateral calculation, or debt tracking, often through secondary or unprotected methods, to obtain undue profits or circumvent solvency controls (CertiK, 2024).

Decimal Miscalculation Exploit: A vulnerability in smart contracts that exploits inconsistencies in the treatment of decimals, particularly errors in scaling factors, conversions between tokens with different accuracies (e.g., 6 vs. 18 decimals), or imperfect rollovers, to manipulate the value of assets, loans, or collateral. This exploit can lead to the unintentional creation of excess tokens, distortion of economic valuations in DeFi protocols, and misappropriation of funds, without violating formal contract rules (Hu et al., 2023).

Delegatecall Exploit: An exploit in which an attacker leverages Solidity's delegatecall function to execute external code while maintaining the storage context of the calling contract, gaining unauthorized access to critical variables, modifying the contract state, or performing malicious functions, often in proxy or upgradeable environments (Zhou et al., 2023).

Deployer Wallet Compromised: A vulnerability in which the wallet that deployed a smart contract is breached, allowing third parties to make unauthorized changes, steal funds, or manipulate critical protocol functions (Carter et al., 2021).

Deposit Function Exploit: Vulnerabilities in which the deposit function (deposit()) in a DeFi protocol is manipulated or exploited to obtain excess assets, alter the internal state of the contract, or circumvent economic constraints, often through decimal errors, atomic interactions, or lack of validation (Zhou et al., 2023).

Dev Privilege Oversight Exploit: Vulnerabilities in DeFi protocols where developer wallets or deployers with special privileges are not properly revoked, audited, or decentralized, allowing for potential unauthorized contract or protocol manipulation (Carter et al., 2021).

DNS Spoofing: Attacks in which DNS infrastructure is manipulated to redirect the user to a malicious version of the front-end or other external services. It can lead to key or asset theft (Zhou et al., 2023).

Donation Attack: Vulnerabilities in which an attacker artificially modifies the flow of funds to a contract, for example, by sending tokens without going through official functions, to manipulate internal state, alter accounting logic, or achieve cost-free profits by exploiting the fact that the contract calculates assets via balanceOf rather than internal accounting (Kong et al., 2025).

Drain vaults: Exploits in which an attacker drains funds held in a DeFi vault by abusing privileged logic, unsafe withdrawal mechanisms, or other contract-level flaws that enable unauthorized token outflows, thereby undermining the protocol's economic security (Su et al., 2023).

Drained Contracts: DeFi smart contracts that, due to exploits, logic bugs, or unrevoked privileges, are emptied of their stored funds, compromising the economic security of the protocol (Qian et al., 2023).

Drained User Wallets: User wallets that are completely emptied following attacks such as phishing, malicious permissions, or interactions with smart contract drainers, often without the user immediately noticing (Qian et al., 2023).

Drained Liquidity Pool: A condition in which a DeFi liquidity pool is emptied of its assets due to exploits such as price manipulation, reentrancy, or flash loan abuse, compromising the protocol's ability to facilitate trading or lending (Qian et al., 2023).

Duplicate Call Exploit: A vulnerability in which an attacker repeats the same call to a sensitive function (e.g., withdraw(), claimReward(), mint()) multiple times within the same transaction or sequentially, exploiting the absence of state checks, idempotence, or logical blocks, to gain unauthorized multiple assets or privileges (Qian et al., 2023).

Empty Market Exploit: A vulnerability in which an attacker interacts with a DeFi market devoid of liquidity or assets, manipulating economic conditions (prices, reserves, exchanges) in the absence of opposition or reaction, to obtain undue profits by leveraging composability and protocol automation (Zhou et al., 2023).

Exploit Lack of Input Authentication: Vulnerabilities in which a smart contract accepts input from unverified or unauthorized sources, allowing attackers to invoke sensitive functions, manipulate internal state, or bypass security checks, leveraging the lack of validation on parameters, addresses, or roles (Wang et al., 2022).

Exploit Weak Authentication Check: A vulnerability in which a DeFi contract applies insufficient or poorly structured authentication checks, allowing attackers to perform restricted functions or modify protocol state, without rigorously verifying the caller's identity or role (Wang et al., 2022).

External Call Vulnerability: A vulnerability in which a smart contract makes calls to external contracts (call, send, delegatecall) without properly handling exceptions, return values, or reentrancy, exposing itself to asset losses, logical manipulations, or unmanaged state failures (Li et al., 2022).

Fake Collateral Exploit: Vulnerability in which an attacker presents false, illiquid, or manipulated assets as collateral (collateral) to obtain loans, liquidity, or economic privileges from a DeFi protocol, exploiting the lack of rigorous checks on the validity, provenance, or valuation of the collateral (Carpentier-Desjardin et al., 2025).

Fee Overflow Exploit: Vulnerabilities in which a DeFi protocol incorrectly calculates or handles fees (fees) via unsecured arithmetic operations, resulting in numerical overflows or precision truncations, which allow attackers to manipulate the balance sheet, circumvent economic limits, or extract unauthorized assets (Sun et al., 2021).

fillQuote silo.borrow() Exploit: An exploit in which an attacker manipulates the fillQuote() function within the silo.borrow() module, exploiting overly permissive approvals and a lack of validation on external inputs, to obtain unauthorized loans or undue assets, isolating the attack from the main protocol.

Flashloan Burn Function Exploit: An exploit in which an attacker uses a flash loan to acquire temporary assets and invokes an unsecured burn() function, altering the state of the DeFi protocol (e.g., supply, balance sheets, rewards) to gain undue economic benefits or cause systemic instability (Alhaidari et al., 2025).

Flashloan Donate Function Logic Exploit: An exploit in which an attacker uses a flash loan to acquire temporary assets and invokes a poorly designed donate() function, exploiting the lack of checks on the provenance, quantity, or legitimacy of the donation, to alter the protocol state, gain undue economic privileges, or activate unintended mechanisms (Alhaidari et al., 2025).

Flashloan Exploit: An exploit in which an attacker uses a flash loan (i.e., an instant, unsecured loan) to manipulate the state of a DeFi contract within a single atomic transaction, exploiting logical vulnerabilities (e.g., lack of controls, reentrancy, overflow) to extract assets or alter economic conditions before repaying the loan (Qian et al., 2023).

Flashloan Governance Attack: An exploit in which an attacker uses a flash loan to temporarily acquire a significant amount of tokens with voting power, and manipulates the on-chain governance of a DeFi protocol (e.g., proposal approval, contract upgrades, fund transfers), exploiting the lack of checks on the quorum, duration, or legitimacy of voting (Alhaidari et al., 2025).

Flashloan Incentive Rewards Exploit: An exploit in which an attacker uses a flash loan to simulate artificial economic participation and activate reward or incentive mechanisms (e.g., staking, liquidity mining, governance), exploiting the lack of verification of the duration, legitimacy, or provenance of funds, obtaining undeserved rewards in a single atomic transaction (Alhaidari et al., 2025).

Flashloan Misconfiguration Exploit: An exploit in which an attacker uses a flash loan to interact with poorly configured functions of a DeFi smart contract (e.g., permissions, approvals, roles), exploiting the absence of logical verification or access restrictions, to alter the protocol state and obtain unauthorized assets in a single atomic transaction (Alhaidari et al., 2025).

Flashloan New Market Exploit: An exploit in which an attacker uses a flash loan to interact with a newly created or poorly configured DeFi market, exploiting the lack of liquidity, validation checks, or logical protections, to obtain unauthorized assets, manipulate initial parameters, or alter the economic state of the protocol in a single atomic transaction (Alhaidari et al., 2025).

Flashloan Pool Shares Exploit: An exploit in which an attacker uses a flash loan to temporarily acquire shares in a liquidity pool and exploits a poorly designed function that assigns rewards, governance, or economic privileges based on the amount of shares held, resulting in undue benefits in a single atomic transaction (Alhaidari et al., 2025).

Flashloan Price Oracle Attack: Manipulation of price oracles (systems that provide quotes) through AMM pool operations, exploited to deceive a protocol (e.g. lending) and obtain assets incorrectly (Cao et al., 2021).

Flashloan Reentrancy Attack: Attacks that exploit flash loans. A vulnerability in smart contracts is exploited to repeatedly call a function before its state is properly updated (Cao et al., 2021).

Flashloan Slippage Attack: An exploit in which an attacker uses a flash loan to manipulate the slippage control function of a DeFi protocol, exploiting the absence of bounds or validations on exchange parameters, to obtain assets under favorable conditions or cause systemic losses in a single atomic transaction (Alhaidari et al., 2025).

Flashloan Swap Logic Exploit: An attack that exploits automated exchange logic (swap) in an Automated Market Maker (AMM) protocol to temporarily alter the exchange ratio between two tokens, thus gaining economic benefits from a flash loan in a single transaction (Cao et al., 2021).

Flashloan Trove Manipulation: Exploits in which an attacker uses a flash loan to manipulate the state of a trove (debt units and collaterals in DeFi protocols such as Liquity), exploiting poorly designed functions or the absence of logical validations, to obtain overborrowing, forced liquidations, or alterations to the collateralization system in a single atomic transaction (Alhaidari et al., 2025).

Flashloan Withdraw Logic Exploit: an exploit in which an attacker uses a flash loan to interact with a poorly designed withdraw() function, exploiting the absence of checks on approvals, roles, or contract state to withdraw unauthorized assets within a single atomic transaction (Alhaidari et al., 2025).

Frontend Attack: an attack in which an attacker compromises or clones the user interface (frontend) of a DeFi protocol, tricking users into signing malicious transactions, interacting with fake smart contracts, or unknowingly transferring assets, by exploiting trust in the graphical interface and the lack of user-side verification (Zhou et al., 2023).

Front-end Vulnerability: a vulnerability in which an attacker compromises or manipulates the user interface (frontend) of a DeFi protocol, inducing users to sign malicious transactions, interact with fake contracts, or transfer assets unknowingly, exploiting trust in the graphical interface (Zhou et al., 2023).

Governance Exploit: an exploit in which an attacker manipulates on-chain governance mechanisms (e.g., voting, quorum, delegation, contract ownership) to gain control over critical protocol functions, such as fund transfers, contract upgrades, or economic parameter changes, exploiting centralized design, lack of timelocks, or poor governance token distribution management (Ma, 2023).

Guardian 2FA Service Exploit: an exploit in which an attacker compromises the two-factor authentication (2FA) service associated with the Guardian wallet recovery system, impersonating the legitimate user to authorize a wallet ownership reset and withdraw unauthorized assets, exploiting the presence of a single guardian or an unverified official guardian (Wang et al. 2022).

Hot Wallet Hack: an exploit in which an attacker compromises an Internet-connected wallet (hot wallet) by exploiting vulnerabilities in private key management systems, web interfaces, or signing services, gaining unauthorized access to digital assets and transferring them to attacker-controlled addresses.

IBC Hooks Exploit: an exploit in which an attacker leverages a reentrancy vulnerability in the logic of IBC hooks (Inter-Blockchain Communication), manipulating IBC channel timeouts to duplicate funds or bypass security checks in an atomic and repeatable sequence, causing systemic losses across interoperable blockchains.

Incentive Rewards Exploit: an exploit in which an attacker simulates artificial economic participation to trigger reward mechanisms (e.g., staking, liquidity mining, governance), exploiting vulnerabilities in incentive systems such as instant snapshots, lack of lockups, or temporal validations, obtaining unearned rewards within a single atomic transaction (Qin et al., 2021).

Incentives Function Mistake: a design error in the economic incentive mechanisms of a DeFi protocol, where the function assigning rewards or penalties does not correctly reflect the intended behavior, causing systemic losses, opportunistic behavior, or economic imbalances between users and liquidators (Qin et al., 2021).

Inconsistent Value in Code: a logical or implementation error in a DeFi smart contract in which economic values or critical parameters (e.g., collateral ratio, reward rate, token balance) are inconsistent across different functions, states, or conditions, leading to unexpected behavior, security vulnerabilities, or failures in liquidation and incentive mechanisms (Qin et al., 2021).

Infinite Mint and Dump: an exploit in which an attacker manipulates the minting function of a smart contract to generate an unlimited amount of tokens beyond the intended cap and rapidly sells them on the market (dump), causing artificial inflation, price collapse, and systemic losses for users and the protocol.

Inflationary Accounting Manipulation: an exploit in which an attacker manipulates accounting variables or calculation logic within a DeFi smart contract to artificially inflate the value of assets, rewards, or collateral, obtaining excessive loans, unearned rewards, or access to privileged functions by exploiting inconsistencies between internal state and real economic value (Wu et al., 2025).

Liquidation Logic Exploit: an exploit in which an attacker manipulates or exploits logical errors in a DeFi protocol's liquidation function, obtaining undue profits, unjustified liquidations, or systemic losses by exploiting calculation inconsistencies, static parameters, or missing validations (Qin et al., 2021).

Liquidity Pool Exploit: an exploit in which an attacker manipulates or exploits vulnerabilities in liquidity pools (LPs) of DeFi protocols to siphon assets, distort prices, or extract undue value, leveraging flaws in smart contracts, swap logic, or incentive mechanisms (Qin et al., 2021).

Liquidity Pools Compromised: a situation in which a DeFi liquidity pool is compromised due to smart contract vulnerabilities, economic manipulation, or fraudulent strategies, leading to fund theft, price distortion, or systemic losses for users and protocols (Qin et al., 2021).

Log Spoofing: an exploit in which an attacker manipulates or forges transaction logs generated by smart contracts (events), causing wallets, DApps, or off-chain bridges to interpret false actions as legitimate, exploiting implicit trust in on-chain logs to obtain assets, alter balances, or deceive users (Liu et al., 2025).

Malicious Governance Proposal: a strategy in which an attacker accumulates voting power (e.g., via flash loans or governance tokens) to submit and pass a malicious proposal that alters the state of a DeFi protocol to transfer funds, change critical parameters, or gain privileged access, exploiting the absence of timelocks, weak quorum requirements, or centralized governance (Ma et al., 2023).

Malicious transfer() Method: a technique in which a smart contract abuses or forges the transfer() function to simulate legitimate fund movements, deceive wallets, DApps, or off-chain bridges, or conceal fraudulent activity, exploiting code obfuscation, fake events, and manipulated addresses (Tan et al., 2025).

Market-Making Bot Exploit: an exploit in which an attacker manipulates the behavior of market-making bots (e.g., algorithmic AMMs or DEX trading bots) to obtain undue profits, exploiting asymmetric information, price adjustment latency, or the absence of reliable oracles, causing the bot to quote incorrect or uncompetitive prices (Nadkarni et al., 2024).

Math Mistake Exploit: an exploit in which an attacker leverages mathematical or calculation errors within a DeFi smart contract, such as overflows, underflows, incorrect rounding, division by zero, or improperly implemented formulas, to gain unfair economic advantages, manipulate balances, or bypass security controls (Zhou et al., 2023).

MEV Bot Manipulation Exploit: an exploit in which a MEV (Maximal Extractable Value) bot manipulates the ordering or structure of blockchain transactions (e.g., on Ethereum), exploiting mempool latency, AMM algorithms, and gas fee prioritization to extract undue value from unsuspecting users, often via front-running, back-running, or sandwich attacks (Choi et al., 2024).

Migrate Function Mistake Exploit: an exploit in which an attacker exploits logical or access-control errors in the migrate() function of a smart contract, designed to transfer state, funds, or configurations between protocol versions, gaining unauthorized access, modifying critical parameters, or draining assets, often in proxy-based or upgradeable environments (Engholm et al., 2025).

Mint Reserves Logic Exploit: an exploit in which an attacker manipulates minting logic tied to a DeFi protocol's reserves, causing the system to issue tokens in excess of the real value of deposited reserves, by exploiting errors in collateralization checks, validation logic, or Loan-to-Value (LTV) calculations (Wen et al., 2024).

Minting Logic Exploit: an exploit in which an attacker manipulates the minting logic of a DeFi smart contract, exploiting errors in calculations, reserve accounting, or validation checks to obtain excess tokens, devalue assets, or drain funds, often through atomic transaction sequences that alter the protocol's internal balances (Wen et al., 2024).

Misconfiguration: a configuration error in the parameters, roles, or functions of a smart contract or DeFi protocol that compromises security, economic logic, or governance, exposing the system to exploits, systemic losses, or unintended behavior (Zhou et al., 2023).

Missing Access Control: a vulnerability in which a smart contract fails to properly implement access controls on critical functions (e.g., mint(), upgrade(), withdraw()), allowing anyone to invoke them and resulting in fund drainage, contract state modification, or execution of restricted operations (Zhou et al., 2023).

Missing Condition Check: a vulnerability in which a smart contract does not correctly verify critical conditions before executing a function, enabling unintended behavior, unauthorized access, or state manipulation, often due to missing require() statements, incomplete logical validation, or absent sanity checks (Zhou et al., 2023).

Missing Input Validation: a vulnerability in which a smart contract fails to properly validate inputs received from users or external contracts, enabling unintended behavior, logical manipulation, or unauthorized access, often due to missing checks on type, format, range, or authorization (Munir et al., 2023).

Oracle Exploit: an exploit in which an attacker manipulates or exploits vulnerabilities in the oracle (external data source) used by a DeFi protocol to artificially alter asset prices, trigger liquidations, obtain excessive loans, or extract undue profits, exploiting reliance on untrusted sources, misconfigurations, or lack of cross-validation mechanisms (Zhou et al., 2023).

Oracle Manipulation: an exploit in which an attacker manipulates the external data source (oracle) used by a DeFi protocol to artificially alter asset prices, triggering liquidations, loans, rewards, or trades to their advantage, exploiting reliance on unreliable sources or misconfigurations (Zhou et al., 2023).

Oracle Misconfiguration Exploit: an exploit in which an attacker takes advantage of incorrect or incomplete oracle configuration in a DeFi protocol to manipulate asset prices, alter economic conditions, or fraudulently trigger liquidation or reward mechanisms (Zhou et al., 2023).

Outdated Oracle Exploit: an exploit in which an attacker leverages stale data provided by an oracle to manipulate the behavior of a DeFi smart contract, obtaining excessive loans, unjustified liquidations, or favorable swaps, due to the protocol's failure to verify data freshness or reliability (Zhou et al., 2023).

OverPaper Function Exploit: a potential exploit in which an overPaper() function or similar allows an attacker to access, duplicate, or export exam content or confidential documents, exploiting access control flaws, missing checks, or insecure distribution logic, such as in BYOD eExam systems (Dawson, 2016).

Over-ride Logic Exploit: an exploit in which an attacker overrides or bypasses the intended logic of a smart contract by exploiting poorly protected functions, delegatecall usage, insecure upgrades, or missing access controls, resulting in unintended behavior, state modification, or fund drainage (Zhou et al., 2023).

Ownership Override Attack: an exploit in which an attacker overrides or takes control of the ownership of a smart contract or DeFi protocol, exploiting missing access controls, unprotected transferOwnership() functions, or initialization logic errors, thereby gaining unauthorized administrative privileges (Zhou et al., 2023).

Price Manipulation Attack: an exploit in which an attacker manipulates the price of a DeFi asset (e.g., token or stablecoin) by exploiting vulnerable market mechanisms, outdated oracles, or AMM algorithms, to obtain undue profits, excessive loans, or favorable swaps, often using flash loans and atomic transactions (Qian et al., 2023).

Price Oracle Attack: an exploit in which an attacker manipulates the price of an asset used by a DeFi protocol by exploiting vulnerable on-chain oracles (e.g., Uniswap-based oracles), to obtain excessive loans, unjustified liquidations, or favorable swaps, often via flash loans and atomic transactions (Qin et al., 2021).

Price Oracle Manipulation: an exploit in which an attacker manipulates the price of an asset used by a DeFi protocol by exploiting vulnerable on-chain oracles (e.g., Uniswap-based oracles), to obtain excessive loans, unjustified liquidations, or favorable swaps, often via flash loans and atomic transactions (Qin et al., 2021).

Private Key Compromised: a vulnerability in which an attacker gains access to the private key of a DeFi user, operator, or administrator, enabling unauthorized access, protocol state manipulation, or direct fund drainage, often through phishing, malware, or operational security failures (Zhou et al., 2023).

Private Key Compromised (Bad ECDSA Implementation): an exploit in which a flawed implementation of the ECDSA (Elliptic Curve Digital Signature Algorithm) generates weak, repeated, or predictable nonces, allowing an attacker to reconstruct the private key from one or more digital signatures and compromise the entire wallet or DeFi protocol (Zhou et al., 2023).

Private Key Compromised (Brute Force): an exploit in which an attacker recovers a private key through brute-force attacks by attempting all possible passphrases, seeds, or cryptographic keys, often enabled by insecure storage, weak passwords, or lack of rate limiting on wallets or RPC interfaces (Zhou et al., 2023).

Private Key Compromised (Discord Hack): an exploit in which an attacker obtains the private key of an operator or moderator through compromised credentials on communication platforms (e.g., Discord), gaining unauthorized access to wallets, smart contracts, or official channels, leading to fund drainage, malicious link dissemination, or governance manipulation (Zhou et al., 2023).

Private Key Compromised (Malware): an exploit in which an attacker acquires a private key from a DeFi user or operator via malicious software (e.g., malware, trojans, keyloggers, infostealers) installed on local devices or servers, enabling unauthorized access, smart contract manipulation, or direct fund theft (Zhou et al., 2023).

Private Key Compromised (Phishing): an exploit in which an attacker obtains a private key from a DeFi user, operator, or administrator using phishing techniques, tricking the victim into revealing sensitive credentials (e.g., seed phrase, private key, passwords) through malicious links, fake interfaces, or deceptive messages, resulting in unauthorized access to wallets or smart contracts (Zhou et al., 2023).

Private Key Compromised (Session Signer): an exploit in which an attacker gains access to a private key or temporary signing session used by a wallet or smart contract to authenticate transactions, exploiting insecure interfaces, persistent sessions, or excessive permissions, leading to unauthorized access, malicious transaction signing, or fund drainage (Zhou et al., 2023).

Private Key Compromised (Social Engineering): an exploit in which an attacker induces a victim to reveal their private key or sensitive credentials through psychological manipulation, deception, or impersonation of trusted entities, using channels such as Discord, Telegram, email, fake websites, or counterfeit wallet interfaces (Zhou et al., 2023).

Private Key Compromised (Stored Publicly): an exploit in which a private key is inadvertently exposed in a public repository, configuration file, container image, or web interface, allowing an attacker to directly access a wallet or contract, resulting in fund drainage, state modification, or assumption of administrative roles (Zhou et al., 2023).

Private Key Compromised (Supply Chain Attack): an exploit in which an attacker obtains the private key of a DeFi wallet or smart contract through a software supply chain compromise, exploiting malicious libraries, tampered development tools, infected public repositories, or manipulated update mechanisms, leading to unauthorized access, malicious transaction signing, or protocol state modification (Zhou et al., 2023).

Private Key Compromised (Unknown Method): an exploit in which a private key is compromised without a clearly identifiable cause, but with observable effects such as unauthorized access, malicious transaction signing, or protocol state modification, suggesting a possible supply chain flaw, human error, backdoor, or undisclosed attack vector (Zhou et al., 2023).

Private Key Compromised (Vanity Address): an exploit in which a private key is compromised due to the generation of a vanity (custom) address using brute-force techniques or insecure tools, exposing the key to collisions, cryptographic weaknesses, or nonce reuse, resulting in unauthorized access, malicious transaction signing, or fund drainage (Zhou et al., 2023).

Proof Verifier Bug: an error within an automated verification system that compromises the validity of formal proofs, causing potentially vulnerable programs or contracts to be incorrectly accepted as safe (Correnson et al., 2023).

Proxy Upgrade Skim: a fraudulent scheme in which a developer upgrades the logic of a proxy contract with malicious code while retaining the same address, diverting funds or assuming controls not anticipated by users (Sun et al., 2025).

Redeem Function Exploit: a vulnerability in which the redeem function is manipulated to obtain more funds than intended, exploiting logical flaws, inaccurate calculations, or insufficient contract state checks (Su et al., 2023).

Redeem Process Exploit: a vulnerability in which the entire redeem process, instead of a single function, is exploited in a sequential or compositional manner to extract more funds than due, leveraging flawed logic, missing checks, or unintended interactions among multiple smart contracts (Su et al., 2023).

Redeem Rounding Error Exploit: a vulnerability caused by bidirectional rounding errors during conversions between collateral and liquidity. An attacker can repeatedly loop trades to exploit minimal discrepancies (e.g., 1 wei) and accumulate undue profits.

Redirected Deposits: an exploit in which user deposits are redirected to unauthorized or attacker-controlled addresses, with the root cause not immediately identifiable. Observable effects include missing funds, anomalous fund flows, or transfers to unexpected contracts, suggesting vulnerabilities in routing logic, proxy configuration, or off-chain infrastructure such as Web3 interfaces or forwarding backends (Zhang et al., 2024).

Reentrancy: a smart contract vulnerability that allows a function to be called recursively before the contract's state is properly updated, potentially enabling repeated or unauthorized use of resources (Qian et al., 2023).

Referral Claims Logic Exploit: a vulnerability in which the logic governing referral reward claims is poorly designed or incomplete, allowing attackers to repeatedly or opportunistically invoke the claim function to obtain illegitimate rewards (Boner, 2023).

Refund Logic Exploit: an exploit in which the protocol's refund logic allows multiple or unauthorized refunds despite unmet conditions, due to insufficient state checks, missing time limits, or weak identity and transaction context verification, indicating an architectural flaw or incomplete oversight of the refund workflow.

Replay Attack: an exploit in which a valid and previously authorized message is intercepted and resent by an attacker to replicate a legitimate action, such as a transaction or authentication, resulting in duplicated operations, unauthorized access, or fraudulent transfers, due to missing replay protection mechanisms such as timestamps, nonces, or session tokens (NIST, 2025).

Resolver Hijack: the overwriting or manipulation of a reference to an external module, such as a resolver, redirecting execution to an attacker-controlled contract (Shou et al., 2024).

Rounding Donation Attack: an exploit in which an attacker donates tokens directly to a smart contract, altering its balance in a way that affects rounding-based calculations such as share distribution or asset conversion. The effects include artificial share inflation, disproportionate allocations, or exchange rate manipulation, indicating a vulnerability in accounting logic that relies on balanceOf rather than dedicated internal variables (Hans, 2025).

Router Exploit: an exploit in which an attacker compromises a router or network component by exploiting known vulnerabilities or misconfigurations, resulting in unauthorized access, traffic interception, DNS modification, or installation of malicious firmware.

Router Exploit via Infinite Approvals: an exploit in which a DeFi router is abused through unlimited (infinite) approvals granted by users, allowing an attacker to invoke unintended functions, perform fraudulent transfers, or intercept multi-hop calls. Observable effects include fund drainage, unauthorized swaps, or malicious cross-chain interactions, indicating flaws in ERC-20 permission management, aggregator router design, or protection against arbitrary call injection (Zhang et al., 2025).

Safe Multisig Wallet Phishing Exploit: an exploit in which an attacker tricks a victim into interacting with a seemingly legitimate multisig wallet that is configured with malicious signers or controlled by external actors, resulting in fund lockup, irreversible asset loss, or unintentional signing of harmful transactions (Su et al., 2023).

Signature Exploit: an exploit in which a valid digital signature is reused, manipulated, or coerced to authorize illegitimate operations on a DeFi protocol, with observable effects such as duplicated transactions, unauthorized access, or fraudulent function calls. The root cause may lie in ECDSA signature malleability, incomplete validation of signature parameters (v, r, s), or the absence of replay and injection protections, indicating a flaw in validation logic or nonce management (Wu, 2025).

Social Engineering (Phishing): an attack in which an adversary manipulates a user's perception or behavior, leveraging external channels such as web interfaces, email, or social media to induce the victim to sign malicious transactions, disclose private keys, or interact with fake smart contracts, exploiting trust in the interface or the DeFi protocol's brand (Zhou et al., 2023).

Spoof Token Exploit: an exploit in which an attacker creates or impersonates a fake token that replicates the interface (ABI) and characteristics of a legitimate token, causing protocols, users, or aggregators to recognize it as valid. The effects include fraudulent swaps, nonexistent credits, or manipulation of DEX indexing, indicating weaknesses in token origin verification, contract validation, or cross-contract approval handling (Zhou et al., 2023).

Staking Logic Exploit: an exploit in which the logic governing staking in a DeFi protocol is manipulated to obtain illegitimate rewards, evade penalties, or alter contract state, without an immediately identifiable cause. Observable effects include fraudulent yield accumulation, lock-up condition evasion, or manipulation of share calculations, suggesting vulnerabilities in internal state management, staking parameter validation, or interactions between derivative tokens and smart contracts (Zhou et al., 2023).

Storage Misalignment Exploit: an exploit in which an attacker leverages a mismatch between the expected and actual memory layout of a smart contract, causing incorrect reads or writes to state data. Effects include unauthorized access to sensitive variables, contract state corruption, or execution of unintended logic, indicating vulnerabilities in storage slot management, delegatecall usage, or interactions between contracts with incompatible layouts (Zhou et al., 2023).

Storage Slot Exploit: an exploit in which an attacker abuses improper storage slot management in a smart contract to access, overwrite, or manipulate sensitive variables, leading to privilege escalation, state corruption, or asset theft (Ruaro et al., 2024).

Swap Function Exploit: an exploit in which an attacker manipulates the swap function of a DeFi protocol to gain undue economic advantages, such as fund drainage, double-counting liquidity, or bypassing price controls. Observable effects include pool balance distortion, artificial trading conditions, or tick range manipulation, indicating flaws in price calculation logic, concentrated liquidity handling, or internal contract arithmetic (Yaish et al., 2023).

Token Approval Exploit: an exploit in which an attacker abuses the approved function of ERC-20 or ERC-721 standards to gain unauthorized access to a user's tokens. The effects include wallet drainage, fraudulent swaps, or illegitimate transfers, often caused by unlimited (infinite) approvals or deceptive interfaces that trick users into signing malicious transactions (Ren et al., 2024).

Transfer Logic Exploit: an exploit in which token transfer logic within a smart contract is manipulated to trigger unintended effects, such as automatic swaps, unnecessary burns, or pool balance distortion. The consequences include price manipulation, liquidity drainage, and fund losses, indicating vulnerabilities in the implementation of transfer, transferFrom, or swap functions, often tied to poorly designed or unprotected automated mechanisms (Wen et al., 2024).

Transferred Treasury to Mixers: an exploit or fraudulent behavior in which a DeFi protocol's treasury funds are moved to mixing services (such as Tornado Cash or Railgun) to obfuscate transaction traceability and conceal fund origins and destinations. The effects include permanent loss of community funds, irrecoverability, and strong indicators of a rug pull or exit scam (Harvey et al., 2024).

Transient Storage Collision: a vulnerability that arises when two Ethereum smart contracts access the same transient storage space introduced by EIP-1153 while using incompatible data layouts for reading and writing (Ruaro et al., 2024).

Trusted Root Exploit: a cyberattack that compromises the "Root of Trust," the immutable hardware or software component used to verify system integrity during the boot process. The exploit allows an attacker to bypass secure boot procedures and gain privileged access by manipulating code executed before the trust chain is established (Zimmer et al., 2016).

Unchecked FlashLoan Approve Exploit: an attack that exploits a logical vulnerability in DeFi contracts where token approvals (approve) granted during a flash loan transaction are not properly revoked or checked. This allows an attacker to retain spending rights over funds that have already been repaid or invalidated, enabling theft within a single atomic transaction (Alhaidari et al., 2025).

Unlimited Repeated Withdrawal Exploit: an exploit that allows a malicious user to repeatedly withdraw funds from a smart contract without their balance being correctly updated, enabling theft of amounts exceeding the available funds (Carter et al., 2021).

Unvalidated Call Data Exploit: an attack against smart contracts that fail to properly validate call data received during operations such as flash loans. This lack of validation allows an attacker to manipulate transaction parameters to execute unauthorized operations, including illicit fund transfers.

User Balances Manually Updated: an attack that exploits manual user balance management in smart contracts, where balance updates are not automated or fully integrated into transaction logic. This vulnerability allows a malicious user to manipulate their apparent or actual balance, enabling multiple or excessive withdrawals beyond the deposited amount (Su et al., 2023).

Vault Swap Exploit: An attack that exploits vulnerabilities in DeFi contracts "vaults" during exchange (swap) operations. By manipulating asset prices through unsecured oracles or interfaces, the attacker can execute favorable transactions, such as opening and closing positions with artificial values, resulting in illicit profits (Wu et al., 2021).

Voting Power Inflation: A phenomenon whereby voting power in a decentralized governance system is artificially increased or concentrated, often through the acquisition of governance tokens, compromising fairness and the democratic distribution of decisions (Barbereau et al., 2022).

Vyper Compiler Bug: Bug in the Vyper compiler (versions 0.2.15, 0.2.16, and 0.3.0) that assigned incorrect memory slots to reentrancy locks, allowing functions marked as @nonreentrant to still be re-invoked at runtime. This exposed smart contracts to vulnerable intermediate states, facilitating reentrancy attacks.

Withdraw Function Argument Manipulation: An attack that exploits the manipulation of withdraw() function arguments in a smart contract. If parameters (such as recipient or amount) are not properly validated, an attacker can alter the logic of the function to withdraw funds from other addresses or obtain amounts greater than the authorized balance (Qin et al., 2021).

WithdrawStuckToken() exploit: An exploit that abuses emergency functions like withdrawStuckToken() to withdraw funds from the contract, often without distinction between locked assets and user deposits. If access is not restricted or tracked, it can turn into an authorized rug pull (Qin et al., 2021).

Appendix B: Platforms and Attacks

This section presents the complete dataset of DeFi platforms that were attacked between 2016 and 2025, as documented by the DefiLlama platform.

Platform	Incidents (N)	Share of incidents (%)	Total loss (USD mln)	Share of total loss (%)	Average loss per incident (USD mln)
Ethereum	184	47.92	7351.826	62.84	39.956
BSC	43	11.20	983.126	8.40	22.863
Arbitrum	28	7.29	76.253	0.65	2.723
Solana	15	3.91	555.495	4.75	37.033
Multi-chain (non-Ethereum)	13	3.39	282.180	2.41	21.706
Polygon	10	2.60	79.609	0.68	7.961
Avalanche	9	2.34	97.420	0.83	10.824
Base	9	2.34	35.785	0.31	3.976
Blast	6	1.56	71.750	0.61	11.958
Optimism	6	1.56	66.100	0.56	11.017
Fantom	6	1.56	61.313	0.52	10.219
zkSync Era	5	1.30	11.322	0.10	2.264
Mixin	2	0.52	222.000	1.90	111.000
Terra	2	0.52	92.000	0.79	46.000
Stacks	2	0.52	12.673	0.11	6.337
Gnosis Chain	2	0.52	11.700	0.10	5.850
Hedera	2	0.52	2.515	0.02	1.258
Cronos	2	0.52	2.250	0.02	1.125
NEM	1	0.26	534.000	4.56	534.000
Bitcoin	1	0.26	305.000	2.61	305.000

(continued)

L. Barbaro et al., *Crypto and Decentralized Finance Under Stress*, SpringerBriefs in Finance, https://doi.org/10.1007/978-3-032-28425-9

(continued)

Platform	Incidents (N)	Share of incidents (%)	Total loss (USD mln)	Share of total loss (%)	Average loss per incident (USD mln)
Sui	1	0.26	223.000	1.91	223.000
Aptos	1	0.26	25.500	0.22	25.500
Starknet	1	0.26	9.550	0.08	9.550
Algorand	1	0.26	9.200	0.08	9.200
Celo	1	0.26	8.400	0.07	8.400
Scroll	1	0.26	7.600	0.06	7.600
Heco	1	0.26	6.000	0.05	6.000
Terra2	1	0.26	5.000	0.04	5.000
PolyNetwork	1	0.26	5.000	0.04	5.000
Loopring	1	0.26	5.000	0.04	5.000
Mode	1	0.26	4.000	0.03	4.000
Fuse	1	0.26	4.000	0.03	4.000
Nervos	1	0.26	3.900	0.03	3.900
Near	1	0.26	3.000	0.03	3.000
Iota	1	0.26	2.350	0.02	2.350
Icon	1	0.26	1.891	0.02	1.891
Harmony	1	0.26	1.750	0.01	1.750
Acala	1	0.26	1.600	0.01	1.600
Mantle	1	0.26	1.400	0.01	1.400
Osmosis	1	0.26	1.100	0.01	1.100
RSK	1	0.26	1.100	0.01	1.100
Abstract	1	0.26	0.400	0.00	0.400
Rootstock	1	0.26	0.150	0.00	0.150
Berachain	1	0.26	0.090	0.00	0.090
Others	12	3.12	514.150	4.39	42.846
Total	384	100.00	11,699.449	100.00	30.467

The manufacturer's authorised representative in the EU is Springer Nature Customer Service Centre GmbH, Europaplatz 3, 69115 Heidelberg, Germany. If you have any concerns regarding our products, please contact ProductSafety@springernature.com

Printed and bound by CPI Group (UK) Ltd, Croydon, CR0 4YY
16/09/2026
02217794-0003